The ZEN Approach™
to Project Management

*Working from your Center to
Balance Expectations and Performance*

George Pitagorsky, PMP

IIL PUBLISHING, NEW YORK

IIL Publishing, New York titles may be purchased in bulk at a discount for educational, business, fund-raising, or sales promotional use. For information, please e-mail michelle. blackley@iil.com or call 212-515-5144.

Published by IIL Publishing, New York a division of International Institute for Learning, Inc., 110 East 59th Street, 31st Floor, New York, NY 10022
www.iil.com

Publisher: Judith W. Umlas
Design: Tony Meisel

Library of Congress Cataloging-in-Publication Data available.

ISBN 0-9708276-9-5

Printed in Canada

Acknowledgments

This book is an expression of gratitude for my incredible good fortune to be immersed in the world of projects while meeting the teachings of the wisdom traditions of Yoga, Taoism, Advaita Vedanta and Buddhism. From these teachings and their application in complex organizations performing complex projects, I am better able to understand the essence of the many attempts to express the nature of our shared experience.

I wish to thank first my wife Linda, a fellow traveler and the loving mirror who helps me to see myself as I am and as I can be.

Thanks to my colleagues at IIL and to E. LaVerne Johnson for publishing this book and for the opportunity to be in the thick of project and quality management with some of the world's great organizations and people. Special thanks to my editors, Judy Umlas and Ed Levy for their contribution to making this expression clear and useful.

Thanks and homage to my teachers from several traditions: Ram Dass and Neem Karoli Baba who taught the essence of loving, serving and remembering and the critical importance of dwelling in the heart; Namkhai Norbu Rimpoche and Tsoknye Rimpoche my teachers in the Tibetan Dzogchen tradition, Chogyam Trungpa Rimpoche who initiated me into the Vajrayana teachings of Tibetan Buddhism with his crystal clarity and crazy wisdom; Jean Klein and J. Krishnamurti with their direct and unrelenting direction to explore the question "who am I?" and cut to the core of self. Thanks also to Gabriel Halpern who introduced me to Yoga and to the joy of chanting and song as a means for going beyond the intellect. Thanks to N.Y. Insight Meditation Center for the opportunity to serve the community as a teacher of meditation and how to apply it in daily life. Thanks also to my children and many friends on the path, too numerous to name but who are a constant support in my inner work and a joyful company in the journey we are on together.

May all beings be happy and find the root of happiness.

Contents

Chapter 1
Managing Your Projects Wisely

A re you awake?

"What a question." You might be thinking, "Of course I'm awake. I'm reading and thinking, am I not?" But what does it mean to be awake in the way that a Buddha is awake?

"Buddha" literally means awakened one, and this book is about what it means to be awake in the way that a Buddha is awake. Of course, it is also about project management and how to do it as well as it can be done. But from the point of view of Zen, managing projects is both a quest in and of itself and a vehicle for awakening. Essentially, we are going to reveal how project management can be used as a Zen art. In Zen there is a tradition of taking apparently mundane daily activities and elevating them into art forms that create paths to spiritual awakening. What makes an activity like project management an art or "Way" is to practice it both for the immediate result and with a view to purifying, calming, and focusing the psycho-physical apparatus—the body-mind complex. The Zen approach will not only benefit your project work tremendously, but it will allow you to extract more personal value from it.

The Zen activity becomes a focal point for concentration as well as a vehicle for addressing all the personal and relationship issues that arise when we are actively trying to accomplish something with a high degree of excellence under challenging circumstances. While perfecting the outer work, important inner work is done, and awakening takes place. This is a book, then, written for people interested in both managing projects and finding a way to reach their highest potential.

Have you ever acted out reactively in response to a wave of emotional feelings? Have you done complex things like driving a car, riding a bike, running on the treadmill or managing a project while *spaced out* to the extent that you have no recollection of how you got to where you are? What did it feel like to wake up and find that you have run a mile on auto-pilot? On the other hand, how does it feel to be completely engaged in an activity while being completely relaxed and aware of everything that is going on in and around you?

Zen is an expression of perennial wisdom. It is a life strategy for managing in an unbounded, unstructured, and groundless field of experience. Are you confused yet?

> "What is the Way?"
> "The Way does not belong to knowing or not knowing. Knowing is illusion. Not knowing is lack of discrimination. When you get to this unperplexed Way, it is like the vastness of space, an unfathomable void, so how can it be this or that, yes or no?"[1]

Going Beyond the Intellect

Zen is about "blowing the mind" out of its normal view. It uses techniques like koans, Zen arts, dialectical argument, self inquiry, and meditation to help the practitioner go beyond his intellect to experience things in an unfiltered way.

All of the methods of Zen attempt to tease you past the confines of the rational, logical mind, past the level of thought, to a much more direct experience of reality. Thus, to understand Zen, it is necessary to abandon all ideology, all presuppositions as to what reality is. In other words, we cannot understand these nonverbal levels by thinking about them; we must simply experience them. As Wendell Johnson points out: "When we have said all we can in describing something, … if asked to go further, we can only point to, or demonstrate, or act out, or somehow exhibit tangibly what we 'mean.'"[2]

"What is the sound of one hand clapping?" is a well known koan. Like all koans there is no intellectual answer. The method is to concentrate on the koan and let go of every attempt at contriving the answer. The answer comes experientially. The process helps to unveil experience from behind the words we use to explain it.

Here is a Zen of project management koan: "When is a project that has no set requirements and no resources complete?"

Another interesting method for going beyond the intellect used in some spiritual traditions is the repetition of the question "Who am I?" Each time you arrive at an answer ("I am Joe, I am Sue's father, I am a manager, I am an American," you ask the question again, and each time an answer is reached, the answerer is confronted with the question: "Who am I?", "Who's asking?" Don't look for the answer intellectually. Just ask, and observe your experience as it goes to deeper levels ("I am a human being," "I am an organism composed of molecules and atoms," "I am Consciousness….")

Of course the power of the intellect as a tool for skillfully living in the world has to be acknowledged. Going beyond the intellect isn't about becoming irrational; it's about getting out of the limited view caused by relying *solely* on our intellect. It is only when we recognize the limitations of the intellect that the intellect can be used most effectively. This is a particularly difficult area for people with strong intellects!

No Ground

Some decades ago it became clear to me that something had removed the ground I was used to standing on from under my feet, and that the structures that I once relied on to guide my life through a neat progression of stages were no longer operating.

How often do you feel, in the midst of your projects, that you are in free fall? The ground is gone. There are no rules. Change is coming so fast that it seems almost impossible to handle it.

Some people just freak out. Others construct elaborate belief systems and structures to create the illusion of stability and protect themselves from the chaos. Others get good at operating joyfully in free fall. We are in in a time in which our beliefs and the structures we have built to protect us from the chaos seem to be breaking down under an onslaught of changing values, conditions, and rational thinking. It seems that the most effective strategy is to get good at feeling comfortable in the free fall state. After all, since there is no ground, we can't really get hurt, so why not enjoy the trip?

Over the centuries, perhaps since the beginning of human consciousness, the greatest, wisest beings have sought to operate effectively and joyously, day to day, in a chaotic world while exploring the underlying reason for being and the essential nature of our existence. Wisdom traditions are found in all cultures and are compatible with any religion. Many believe that these wisdom teachings are really the foundation and source of the world's religions and philosophies.

Seeing Things as They Are

> "Dispassionate objectivity is itself a passion, for the real and for the truth."
>
> **Abraham Maslow[3]**

The Zen approach is founded on the ability to see things as they are. Moment to moment mindfulness, coupled with an inquiry into the nature of how and why things work, are the principle tools. A Zen approach blends a systems-oriented view with the need for dynamic balance and complete accountability and responsibility for one's actions. Zen works to overcome static *either-or* thinking.

The approach uses the right degrees of analysis and intuition; hard and soft skills. It insists that the individual be "centered," skillful, realistic, and sensitive to the needs and behaviors of self and others. It addresses the experiential and behavioral aspects of performing. And it is founded on the understanding that all effective action stems from compassion and lovingkindness based on the realization that everyone is in the same boat.

In this book, the term *Zen* is used to roll together all of these concepts. This is not an orthodox treatment of Zen. The book could have been called the Yoga, Tao, or Way of Managing Projects. In the end all of these terms are pointing to the same basic strategy—regard everything as a part of a holistic, integrated system, set your intention to include all of your personal and nonpersonal goals, apply objectivity and subjectivity in dynamic balance, seek to perfect yourself and your performance while not being hung up about your imperfections, and recognize that a balance between doing and not doing is essential for healthy living in the world.

> The message is: Be mindful, consciously aware, critically analytical, kind and compassionate, focused like a laser, open like the sky, fearless in the face of reality, self-confident, and humble.

Paradox and Balance

> Paradox is the norm when it comes to working with complex concepts and relationships. There are *no* absolutely right answers. We seek the answers that are right for the situation.

Many people want certainty. Clients, project sponsors, project managers, and others all want to know when what they want will be done, how much it will cost, exactly what they have to do, and how to do it. But life is filled with paradox and uncertainty. For those who desire consistent repetition of a well-articulated script, this is disconcerting. For them, deviation from the plan creates discomfort.

Others want no structure. They like to let the future unfold as it will and to creatively adapt to its conditions. They feel that structure gets in the way of creativity and it is unrealistic to tie themselves down.

This division between the structured and unstructured schools of thought is one of many such dichotomies. The knee-jerk reaction to dichotomy is conflict; however, in the wisdom way, we apply the principle of balance, that dynamic state of ease that occurs when all opposing forces are present to the right degree. There is nothing in excess and no insufficiency. As conditions change, the balance is maintained by adjusting the forces—just like balancing on a tight rope. Too rigid or too loose, you fall. Too far to the right or left, you fall. Think too much about it and you fall.

Paradox and dichotomy are words that imply two. In the Zen way there is one; within the one there are many. Balance is among many interacting forces and many possible ideas within that singular whole. The wise think in continuums, not polarities. What is the right point to be at in the continuum at this moment? That is the question we subtly ask to help maintain balance and avoid unnecessary conflict.

Letting Go

The wisdom approach goes beyond thinking. It is about experiencing. It is about simply "letting things happen." Letting things happen is pretty unconventional in the context of project management. After all, projects are about *making* things happen, not *letting* them happen.

How do we let making things happen, happen?

How can we initiate plan, execute, control, and close projects with the highest degree of excellence while *letting go* into the flow that occurs when intention, effort, concentration, mindfulness, and skill are all in proper balance? How can we be dispassionately objective and still address our goals and objectives with the passion required for excellence?

These are the questions to be answered in this exploration of project management from the Zen perspective.

Zen elicits an image of clear, quiet peacefulness, like a beautiful rock garden or a still pond set among pines with a full moon reflected in it. Projects and project management often elicit a very different image—drive, controlled chaos, tight schedules, restrictive budgets, anxiety, conflict, disappointment, accomplishment, value.

Inner and Outer Work

Can these two images be reconciled? How to do we blend Zen and the underlying wisdom it represents with project management and its quest for satisfying people and organizations with valuable outcomes within time and cost constraints?

Blending Zen and project management enables us to more effectively manage projects to get the results we want, when we want them, for the price we expect to pay. This is the outer work—perfecting the form and perfecting its results.

Blending Zen and project management enables us to consciously perfect the form while using whatever we do, in this case managing and working on projects, as a vehicle for overcoming the obstacles that keep us from achieving self-actualization. Self-actualization, in Abraham Maslow's terms, is the *"intrinsic growth of what is already in the organism, or more accurately, of what the organism is."* Reaching full potential, then, comes when an individual eliminates the self-imposed barriers that are blocking it. This quest for self-actualization is the inner work—perfecting the self.

Who This Book Is For

Everyone does projects. They range from the small and simple to the large and complex. Projects are the means for making all improvements, developing new products, putting on events, and anything else that requires work to be done to achieve results within a finite time and cost.

Projects are often more complex and stressful than they need to be. Far too many of them fail to meet expectations. There are far too many conflicts. There are too few moments of joy and too much anxiety. But there is hope. It is possible to remove the unnecessary stress and complexity. This book is about how to do just that. It links the essential principles and techniques of managing projects to a "wisdom" approach for working with complex, people-based activities.

This book is for anyone who manages, works on, or is interested in projects, whether they are certified project management professionals (PMPs) or not. Most people who manage projects in the world are *not* professional project managers. Many are untrained and have little or no professional support. Some do not even know they manage projects; they just get things done. There are professionals who manage large complex projects in global settings and incidental project managers who manage or take part in projects that are part of their normal jobs in just about any field. There are others who manage projects like moving, renovating a kitchen, or putting on a wedding. But everyone can gain value from stepping back to see the big picture objectively, while at the same time retaining that personal perspective that represents one's experience, knowledge, and intuition.

Wisdom

Wisdom is applied experiential knowledge—knowledge beyond intellect—based on an unobstructed, unfiltered view of how things are. It is founded on the ability to accept things as they are as a starting point for meaningful, useful action. This ability to accept things as they are is enabled by working from one's "center"—that calm, objective place from which action flows in a way that is perfectly appropriate to the situation at hand.

Everyone can experience a sense of inner peace. Everyone has the ability to *take a step back* to see things objectively. Doing so makes project success more likely. In fact, that is what managing projects is all about—objectively looking at performance by initiating and planning, by coordinating and controlling, and by closing the project in a way that sets a solid foundation for the future. This same quality of seeing things objectively can be applied to everything we do. Project management becomes a metaphor for how we can live our lives and, if we follow the wisdom traditions, the way we live our lives becomes a metaphor for how to manage projects.

That is not to say that we have to formally plan everything, and keep track of everything we do, and be emotionally shut down. It means that when we are doing whatever we do, we can be aware of our intention and our objectives. We can be aware of why we have our intentions and objectives, of the beliefs that lie behind them. We can be aware of the impact of our actions on achieving what we want to achieve and on the people and things around us. We can be aware of the limited degree to which we actually have control of ourselves, others, and our environment, and the inevitable reality of impermanence, uncertainty, and risk. By being aware of these things, we question everything we do and the beliefs that lead us to do them. This gives us the ability to apply the most skillful means possible to accomplish the most effectively selected ends.

Improve Performance

Stepping back provides the *edge* needed to excel. The Zen approach is about being able to step back without disengaging from the current situation—being simultaneously dispassionately objective *and* passionate. It is about doing the dishes, chopping wood, and carrying water, or writing a weekly status report in a way that makes these mundane activities parts of a fully integrated, joyful, and perfect whole.

This book is about how to improve intrapersonal and interpersonal performance. It is about getting the right projects done right. It explores how to integrate and apply a highly effective personal and project management approach to minimize unnecessary conflict, stress, and disappointment, and to achieve results that meet or exceed expectations.

The book guides readers in exploring how to:

- maintain moment to moment mindfulness to maximize effectiveness;
- use planning and communication techniques to establish and manage realistic expectations, the roots of project success;
- remain calm and energetic while being active and effective in the face of chaos, fear, resistance to change, unrealistic demands, conflict, and the other aspects of project life that cause stress;
- take a systems or holistic perspective to see where projects and the people who perform them fit in their environment, affect it, and are affected by it;
- break free of self-imposed barriers to creative thinking, conflict resolution, and problem solving;
- use day-to-day experiences as opportunities for continuous personal and group improvement.

To be more effective, you have to weave together practical techniques, core "wisdom" concepts, and basic principles of project management; integrate the "scientific," technical side of project management with the interpersonal and intrapersonal behavioral skills that are the real keys to effective performance; and balance the right and left brain to become more effective.

What does it mean to be more effective? It means accomplishing the things you want to get done without excess effort, while making sure they will be useful to the people, including yourself, who are the beneficiaries of your work. Being effective also means integrating your personal life and work life into a whole that includes a quest for self-actualization along with fulfillment of your social, security, recognition, and physiological needs. Being effective is making good use of your time and effort, rather than wasting it on unnecessary and unpleasant pursuits that have no positive payback.

Analysis and Systems View

We will explore Zen and the individual project management elements such as risk, communications, people management, and estimating. These, however, are never found independently in real world projects. Risk is an integral part of estimating and scheduling. Cost and time have a complex relationship with each other and with the quality of results and resources. Communication is a critical enabler for everything we do. Process management and performance improvement are fully integrated with performance itself. What we do today influences what we do tomorrow and how we do it. Zen is integrated into the relative world of people and things.

Subjects may be looked at separately to obtain analytical clarity, but in the end they are all unified in a single system. It is all one. Everything is part of a web of interacting people, places, things, events, thoughts, feelings, and sensations. Everything exists in a complex system in which any action anywhere (note that speech and the decision *not* to act are also actions) has an effect elsewhere, and perhaps everywhere. Therefore, be mindful of what you do and why you do it. Be mindful of the fact that while you can predict the impact of your actions sometimes, you can't predict their impacts all the time. Even when you think you are in control, you aren't.

In addition, complex systems are nonlinear. They do not simply consist of a set of sequential steps. Time and the interplay among the objects and actions in the system create a dynamic, cyclical process. To manage well, therefore, requires *a nonlinear* approach, one that intertwines the various parts into a cohesive whole, like the various strands that make up a strong rope. While the strands may be individually interesting, it is the rope that is of real use. In the same way, projects, like the rest of life, do not unfold neatly in a simple linear progression. Things happen based on causes and conditions. Everything that happens becomes the causes and conditions going forward.

There are complex cycles over time. For example, when we define requirements for a project and base an estimate on them, we invariably find that defining the requirements and delivering an outcome based on what has been defined elicits changes. The client, seeing what he asked for, realizes that it is not really what he wants. The reality of the concrete, delivered outcome is different from the idea he had in mind, and the idea is different from the statement of requirements.

The wise project manager accepts this reality and follows a process that allows for the progressive elaboration of requirements in a way that enables the client to see as concretely as possible the implications of his requirements. As the requirements come closer to being a true reflection of the desired outcome, estimates are modified.

Because projects are human systems and human systems are the most complex, there is no cookbook of ordered steps. There is a useful set of ingredients that are combined to suit the needs of a situation at hand. At the same time there is a comprehensive model that if adapted to the needs of a situation will significantly improve the probability of success. It is possible to learn from experience and it is quite skillful to apply that learning in future efforts, but don't think that anything involving people working across time will consistently repeat itself exactly as it has occurred in the past.

While there is no cookbook approach to project management that works, there is great power in having a repeatable process that is adaptable to current conditions. This is just one of the many paradoxes found in our world of projects and Zen wisdom. We need processes, standards and procedures defined. We need rules. Yet none of them are ever able to truly define the real world.

Paradox is a fact of life in complex systems. Not this, not that, but some combination of the two.

Awareness, Concentration, and Mindful Presence

A Tibetan teacher of mine, Namkhai Norbu Rimpoche[4], considers awareness, concentration, and mindfulness to be foundation elements in the wisdom approach. He gives an example of a normal adult who has a cup of poison in front of him and is aware of it. He knows the danger of poison and can help others be aware of the poison by telling them not to drink from the cup. But some of these others, even though they know of the danger, don't consider it important or have doubts about it. Some may not be aware. For these it is necessary to create a law against drinking from the cup or taking the cup out of their reach, as one would do with a child. These actions can save the lives of irresponsible people, people who lack awareness.

Namkhai Norbu extends the example to include the idea of mindfulness and the concentration needed to remain *present*. Assume that the adult, fully aware of the danger of the poison, forgets. He becomes distracted and loses presence. He is no longer mindful of what is in the cup. Thirsty and without thinking, he may take a sip and die.

With less fatal consequences, we see this operating all the time in projects. Even when we are aware of the danger of making promises without writing them down, or the consequences of changing requirements without documenting, evaluating, and approving them, we are not mindful and do what will cause us grief later. Awareness is knowing or being cognizant of something. Mindfulness is remembering that you know. Mindfulness can be cultivated.

Here is an exercise for cultivating mindfulness and concentration. Right now, you can take a moment to bring yourself to the present moment. Become aware of your body and breath. See how your breath is. Is it calm and long; short; choppy, so subtle you barely feel as if you are breathing? Feel your body against your chair; your feet on the ground. Exhale. Take a second or two to relax, mindful of your body and breath. Then go back to the reading.

If you become aware that you have lost your concentrated mindfulness on your reading (like for example, when you have read a paragraph or, maybe, several pages, but have no idea that you've read it or what was in it) just bring your awareness to your body and breath and begin again.

This is a taste of a core exercise for improving mindfulness and concentration. Doing this over and over again, consciously, trains the mind to be more present. Being more present enables you to be more effective. Try it. It takes less than a minute. In this case you are practicing mindful reading, but you can do it wherever you are; whatever you are doing; whenever you remember. The more you do it the more natural it becomes. The more natural it becomes the more you remember to be present. The more present you are, the more likely you will do the right thing to get your project done well and the more you will be using your work to perfect yourself.

Throughout the book I will remind the reader. I will repeat the question "Are you awake?" and briefly restate this core exercise. The last chapter contains a more formal version of mindfulness practice and an explanation of how it works and how to use it in your life.

Influences and Intention

This book is influenced by my experience in blending business, family, social life and the search for self-actualization. As a business person and householder I have a very realistic sense of what goes on in companies, families, and communities. As a longtime practitioner of Yoga and the nondual teachings of Advaita, and a student, practitioner, and teacher of Buddhist meditation and wisdom, I have had a taste of what seems like "reality."

Early in my experience, it seemed as if the material realms—work, family, organizations, schedules, and the like—were real and the spiritual, ethereal, realms imagined. Then, for a while I thought the reverse was true, that the so called real world was illusion and that the only thing that was real was emptiness and clarity. I have come to learn that

"to deny the reality of things is to miss their reality;
to assert the emptiness of things is to miss their reality.
The more you talk and think about it, the further astray you wander
from the truth.

Stop talking and thinking and there is nothing you will not be able to know. …

Do not search for the truth: only cease to cherish opinions."[5]

We live in the relative world of subjects and objects, yet this world exists in the ground of unbounded absolute emptiness and clarity. While we skillfully can and should use our intellect to operate in the relative world, to achieve self perfection we must transcend the intellect and simply experience things as they are. To get to the truth, it is necessary to see our opinions for what they are, opinions, and to question them objectively.

We collaborate with one another to create an illusion that keeps us stuck in a never-ending cycle of seeking pleasure and avoiding pain. That cycle is fueled by wanting things to be different from the way they are. This book is about how to break free of this cycle to reach self-actualization using the concrete daily work we are immersed in. In the Zen context this means reaching a point at which one awakens to his or her intrinsic nature – wisdom and compassion without boundary. While we are breaking free, we cultivate the qualities of skillful and ethical behavior that help us excel in what we do and make sure that what we do is of real benefit, not only to ourselves but to all beings everywhere.

As we approach this realization, we become experts at moving through life and playing in the illusion. The cycle no longer controls us. We are above it and in it simultaneously. What was once the hardship of living and working becomes a joyous dance. We do what we do expertly.

My wish is that this book be of benefit to anyone who wishes to awaken.

Chapter 2

Wisdom Perspective:
Zen and the Art of Project Management

> "So the thing to do when working on a motorcycle, as in any other task, is to cultivate the peace of mind which does not separate one's self from one's surroundings. When that is done successfully, then everything else follows naturally. Peace of mind produces right values, right values produce right thoughts. Right thoughts produce right actions, and right actions produce work which will be a material reflection for others to see of the serenity at the center of it all."
>
> Robert M. Pirsig, *Zen and the Art of Motorcycle Maintenance*

Purpose

Getting projects done on time and within budget, while delivering a satisfactory outcome, is a challenge. Getting projects done while staying calm, cool, and collected—and learning something about yourself at the same time—increases the challenge exponentially.

A wisdom perspective, coupled with best practices in project management, will provide the edge that improves the probability of success while "cultivating the peace of mind which does not separate one's self from one's surroundings." This is the blending of inner work and outer work that characterizes Zen. Inner work is the cultivation of mindfulness, concentration, and wisdom. The outer work is doing whatever is needed to function in the material world.

The Case of the Stressed-Out Project Manager (PM)

Pat was a PM with ten years of experience in high-stress, sales-driven projects. Her typical project duration ranged from a few weeks to several months. There were always several projects going at the same time. Pat and her team took on all the work they were presented with and generally made their externally set deadlines, but with lots of juggling and heroics. Because of the speed at which they worked, they often cut corners and kept track of things very informally, relying on their ability to remember what they needed to do when they needed to do it. They were good, though occasionally something fell through the cracks.

Pat's team was continually turning over. The brightest of the people she took so much time to get up to speed burned out or realized that the stress was above and beyond their job expectations. Pat herself was beginning to question whether this was the way she wanted to spend her days—and many of her nights.

On her way back from a project management course, she picked up a book on Zen archery and it struck her that the idea of perfecting one's performance could be applied to anything, not just Zen practices like archery, calligraphy, the tea ceremony, and the martial arts. She decided to turn the management of her projects into a Zen exercise. How could she perfect the project process without getting bureaucratic? How could she use her attention to detail to reduce her own stress and the stress on her staff? How could she do just the right amount of planning and controlling while being completely efficient? How could she know when to follow her feelings and when to rely on analysis and intellect? How could she learn more about how she behaves in relationships? And how could she achieve self-actualization without retiring to a monastery or becoming a master archer?

Foundation

Zen cuts through complexity to go straight to the heart of a matter. It promotes *knowing* through inner experience, and discipline from within. In the Zen way, the individual comes to fully know his or her own nature by cutting through intellectualism, cultural barriers, conditioned responses, rules, and any other "extras" that get in the way of being present and objective in each moment. For a brief historical perspective on Zen see Appendix II.

> **"Zen is not some kind of excitement, but concentration on our usual everyday routine. "**
>
> **Shunryu Suzuki[6]**

One who possesses this kind of knowledge has wisdom, and wisdom leads to compassion. We don't create wisdom and compassion. They simply emerge as the conditioning that keeps them obscured drops away. Wisdom and compassion are natural. There is no need to fabricate them.

In Zen one attains direct knowledge of the mind's basic state of unbounded spaciousness and clarity. We recognize this spaciousness and clarity as the basic ground of everything we experience, the space out of which all our thoughts arise. This experience is what some call presence, God consciousness, or enlightenment—although naming it immediately limits it. Discussing it can never replace the experience, just as thinking and talking about a fabulous sunset or a perfect rose can never substitute for the essential experience of them.

The Zen way posits that within this basic ground, as things unfold in day to day life, an individual can modify his/her behavior by becoming mindful of the thoughts, feelings, physical sensations, sights, sounds, tastes, smells, and sights that continuously arise in the field of consciousness. Mindfulness of thoughts is particularly important. The Buddha taught that:

The thought manifests as the word,
The word manifests as the deed,
The deed develops into habits,
And the habit hardens into character.

So watch the thought
And its ways with care,
And let it spring from love
Born out of respect for all beings.[7]

The more one is mindful of the arising of one's thoughts, the more control one has over one's words and actions. One need not be reactive to past conditioning. One can become authentic by making choices rather than being driven by habit. Proactivity replaces reactivity. The practitioner proactively chooses to do no harm and to attempt to do things that are helpful.

The Basic Teachings

Zen's basic teachings are relatively simple.

As humans we experience stress, anxiety, discomfort, and unease caused by our attachments to things that are impossible to attain or keep. In the realm of projects this translates to the pain and suffering caused by driving to meet a delusional deadline, which, if met, would deliver a product of questionable acceptability.

We are constantly grasping the things we want and pushing away what we don't want. But it isn't the wanting or not wanting that causes difficulty, nor is it the things themselves. The problem is attachment or clinging—the attempt to hold on to what is passing and impermanent; and aversion—the pushing away of things that cannot be avoided. These are what cause us pain. In projects we often see how people holding onto their ideas or beliefs when they are out of synch with reality causes avoidable conflict and poor results. We also see resistance to change and avoidance of things, like adhering to planning disciplines or writing things down that are unpleasant. This resistance and avoidance results in poor performance, avoidable conflict, and dissatisfaction.

We suffer when we want things to be different than they <u>can be</u>. We want the new product to be delivered next Tuesday, but the amount of work needed to be done and the availability of the people to do it won't allow it. If we let go of our wanting, we can effectively plan for a realistic and positive outcome. If we cling to the wanting, then all hell breaks loose and we have a mad dash to get it done, usually with a dismal outcome.

But there is hope. We can overcome the tendency to cling and push away when clinging and pushing away are counterproductive.

In Zen, the way to free oneself from conditioned and self-imposed suffering is to follow a path that combines the right measures of wisdom, concentration, and ethical action, using "skillful means"—tools and techniques.

The path of skillful means begins with an exploration of some basic realities. The practitioner experientially verifies the following:

- This life is a rare occurrence.
- Ultimately everything is impermanent; therefore, you are not completely in control, and therefore there is no certainty about how things will turn out.
- We are responsible for our actions and for the results of those actions: what we do affects us and others.
- There is no solid self; the ego is a construct of causes and conditions. It is in constant flux. When you look for it, it cannot be found.

This understanding of the nature of things is the wisdom aspect of the path.

The Zen way is to accept things as they are. Accepting things as they are does *not* mean being passive. We change what can be changed, but to freak out, complain, and mope about the way things are is not skillful. We recognize that we can change neither the past nor the immediate present. Like it or not, we are stuck with them. We can change the future.

In project management we consciously manage risk and uncertainty. We assess the risks, acknowledge the uncertainty, and fold them into the plan. We recognize the limitations of our organization and its management style and do our best. We do our best to get what we want (assuming it is worth the effort) but are realistic about what we can accomplish given the time, resources, and other conditions.

The Zen path includes ethical behavior. The ethical aspects of the path pretty much boil down to do no harm and do things that will help. In the teachings, right speech, right livelihood, and right action are the ethical elements. These are put forth as skillful means to avoid problems and support the quest for self-actualization. Note, that the Project Management Institute's (PMI®) Guide to the Project Management Body of Knowledge (PMBOK® Guide) also highlights ethical behavior as a part of the project manager's professional responsibility.

The remaining part of the path is made up of right effort, concentration, and mindfulness. These focus on cultivating the personal power to work with one's mind and apply this power to effective living.

The path is nonlinear. One works on all aspects simultaneously and they support and reinforce one another. For example, attention to right action helps to strengthen mindfulness and concentration. Mindfulness and concentration enable both the cultivation of right action and wisdom.

Balance

In the Zen way, either/or thinking is eliminated. Instead, we seek a point of balance between apparent opposites. A famous teacher of Zen Buddhism, Alan Watts, wrote about why it's necessary to embrace apparent opposites, using the example of reason and intuition in decision-making:

We feel that we decide rationally because we base our decisions on collecting relevant data on the matter in hand. … Yet [someone] might ask whether we really know what information is relevant, since our plans are constantly upset by unforeseen incidents. . .

In other words, the "rigorously scientific" method of predicting the future can be applied only in special cases where prompt action is not urgent, where the factors involved are largely mechanical, or in circumstances so restricted as to be trivial. By far the greater part of our important decisions depends on a "hunch"—in other words, upon the "peripheral vision" of the mind. Thus the reliability of our decisions rests ultimately upon our ability to "feel" the situation, upon the degree to which this peripheral vision has been developed.[8]

This of course is controversial in PM circles. The analytical scientific school of thought insists that the right data must be presented in the right way and analyzed objectively. The seat-of-the-pants school says that it is all about following your gut, being able to read the current situation and respond, often heroically. When we apply the principle of balance, we see that a blending of the two is what really works in the real world of projects— just the right measures of analysis and intuition to suit the situation.

Project Management As a Means of Self-Inquiry

Project management is a complex discipline. Taken as a means for self-inquiry, it is like martial arts, or a Japanese tea ceremony—an exercise with the goal of perfecting its outer performance while at the same time perfecting one's inner wisdom. In effect we are doing two things at once: following a discipline and using it as a vehicle for self-actualization.

In the wisdom traditions it is recognized that relationships are the most fertile ground for self-actualization. Projects are almost always exercises in relationship. They give us the opportunity to work on ourselves and the way we react rather than respond. They are the place where we can practice mindfulness and concentration and exercise our ethical behavior on our feet. Projects are an opportunity to test our intellectual wisdom so that it becomes *embodied* wisdom, beyond intellect and analysis.

Handling strong feelings is an example of the way self inquiry might work in a project setting. It is usually not good to act out feelings, especially in the workplace, though, of course it is unrealistic to think that strong feelings like anger won't arise. It is healthy to be aware of our reactions to situations and to the arising of our anger or other feelings. This is being mindful. Can you experience the anger, then let it pass and calmly assess the situation so that you can respond skillfully? This inquiry may lead to another, such as what really got you so angry? Why? What can you do about it in your personal quest for self-actualization?

In addition to being able to handle strong feelings without letting them drive behavior, with practice it becomes possible to see the arising of the anger before it manifests itself and to simply let it go and deal with the situation dispassionately. One also begins to see the behaviors that may trigger strong feelings in others, and this enables positive behavioral change.

While a project has a clearly defined outcome, deliverable according to schedule and budget, self-actualization and perfection of the process are more like *Kaizen,* the Japanese management approach of continuous quality improvement. According to Kaizen, perfection is always out of reach, but in making incremental improvements, we are always approaching it.

Doing It

At this point the normal busy person may be thinking, *I barely have time to do all the things I have to do; where will I get the time to play some mind game?*

Not to worry. Self inquiry and the quest for self-actualization do not require extra time, though there is effort involved. There is no need to retire to a monastery or become an archer. No need for deep philosophical discussions. In the Zen way your daily routine is the most fertile ground for self-actualizing. All you have to do is to take on wisdom exercises that you do simultaneously with the task of mindfully attending to what you think and do during your normal work and play, and in your normal relationships.

Wisdom exercises are experiments to test out principles or techniques that are related to the inner work of self-actualization and the outer work of perfecting the form. Wisdom exercises can work on both the inner and outer levels. As described in the first chapter, the inner level focus is on self-actualization. The outer level focus is on continuously improving the process—project management, for example.

As an example, our friend Pat decided to work on getting more organized and formal while keeping relationships natural and flowing and not creating any more work for anyone. At the same time, she wanted to get less stressed and more in control.

She began her wisdom exercise program with the simple step of acknowledging each new project request with an e-mail. She worked out a format and outline and when the sales person called she brought up the 'template' she had made of typical questions and took the sales person through them. Her objective was to make it seem as informal as usual, while making sure she got all the information. She also wanted to see just how disciplined she could be without becoming rigid.

At first, she forgot and fell back into her usual habit of listening, remembering, and passing on the oral information. As soon as she realized that she had forgotten, she called the project initiator back and went through her little questionnaire (though never referring to it as a questionnaire or anything "formal"). It took only a few minutes, so no one really minded.

Her remembering took no time at all. Each time she remembered, it reinforced the process. Each time she remembered, it improved her mindfulness and reminded her that she was sometimes "asleep." It helped her see the difference between being asleep, or falling into habitual behavior, and being awake or mindful of the situation. This is part of the inner work. The questioning is part of the outer work.

Remember the little one-minute exercise from chapter 1? Pat practiced it from time to time as she worked at her desk and attended meetings. A moment of focus on the breath, the physical body, and in most situations she was centered again.

Are you awake? Where is your mind?

After a short time, her ability to give solid, written information to her staff and to keep track of the information made her feel more relaxed. There was less uncertainty. Her head wasn't full of all that information, and the anxiety about forgetting any of it was gone. Her staff and her clients both began to sense greater confidence, and that led to fewer unnecessary phone calls, fewer things falling through the cracks, and more ease in fulfilling requirements. The work on the outer level was paying off.

As Pat realized some success, she added additional disciplines: a simple feedback e-mail to the project initiator with a request for confirmation; clear e-mail subject lines, and documents with the project name and a date to identify versions; some tracking of the time spent on each of the projects; and a simple filing system so she could more easily find what she needed when she needed it.

As she got more organized and disciplined, she continued to experience less anxiety, less confusion, greater clarity, and a higher degree of concentration. She was becoming more energized and calmer. And as she became calmer and continued to practice her PM disciplines, her staff began to follow suit. Not because they had to, but because they saw that it helped to improve the way they worked and because they liked what was happening to Pat.

Mindfulness

Taking on the pursuit of wisdom does not require a significant investment in time. It does require the effort to shift your perception and remain mindful of the way you do your work. It does require self discipline and commitment and the courage to change old ways and replace them with new ones. With the ability to see things more clearly, the distortion caused by one's conditioned, habitual reactions is continually reduced.

> The key to performance is the process. Become mindful of your process—the way you do what you are doing. Recognize that through changing your process, you affect end results. And yet the effects are *not* fully predictable; uncertainty increases with the scope and complexity of the system.

Mindfulness is the quality of being attentive to everything—thoughts, feelings, physical sensations, sights, sounds, smells, tastes—that arises in and around you. Increased mindfulness and concentration reduce stress and enhance the power of the intellect. They make us more capable of responding rather than reacting. Chapter 11, Managing from Your Center, discusses the concept of being centered and provides a simple but profound technique for cultivating mindfulness and concentration. You can read it now (it won't ruin the story!) or wait until you come upon it naturally. If you read it now, you may find it interesting to try practicing the technique while you read the rest of the book. If not, you are again invited to be aware of your body and breath whenever you sense that you have "gotten lost" in your thoughts.

Accepting Uncertainty

The courage to accept uncertainty as a given is intrinsic to the Zen tradition. We live in a very dynamic, some say chaotic, time. Things change moment to moment. We can no longer rely on the comforts of a predictable life in a well marked out area. This is ever increasingly the case with projects. Everything seems to be moving faster and faster. Conditions change, people change their minds, communication is 24/7, the drive to beat the competition is reinforced by the growth in competition, everyone wants what they want as fast as they can get it, or faster.

"This is why, I think, there is a so much interest in a culturally productive way of life which, for some fifteen hundred years, has felt thoroughly at home in 'the Void,' and which not only feels no terror for it but rather a positive delight. To use its own words the situation of Zen has always been—

"Above, not a tile to cover the head;
Below, not an inch of ground for the foot." [9]

What does it mean to not have a tile to cover the head; no ground? There is no protection, no foundation to rely on. Imagine again being in free fall without a ground. You can freak out or enjoy the ride. Since there is no ground, you aren't going to hit anything.

We seek, through mindful awareness, to let go of our desire to control what cannot be controlled and to hold onto what cannot be held onto. We jump into the icy cold water ready to enjoy the shock and the cleansing it will bring.

Applying the Wisdom

Let's see how the Zen approach can be applied in schedule negotiation, a common source of unnecessary stress.

If a project must be done on time, a master project manager will make sure there is a realistic schedule. The practitioner cultivates "the peace of mind which does not separate oneself from one's surroundings" as she negotiates a schedule that acknowledges uncertainty and is based on the practical reality of limited resources and limited control of other peoples' behaviors.

A realistic schedule results from a process that applies technical skills, tools, conflict resolution, negotiation skills, authority and hierarchy, fear of failing and of saying no, communication, and risk assessment, among other elements.

The schedule is crafted the way a potter shapes a vase on the wheel. The PM concentrates, giving herself the time to work at the schedule. The requirements are assessed, tasks to fulfill them are identified, described and estimated, the tasks are logically sequenced. The capacity and availability of resources are assessed and folded into the mix. Uncertainties are identified and considered. Multiple scenarios are explored. The right level of documentation and supporting material is developed.

If the client or manager becomes insistent that the deadline must be met under any circumstances, and the project manager feels that it is impossible, the project manager presents a logical argument, in writing, identifying assumptions, conditions, and facts. He provides alternatives and trade-offs. He builds a case that is presented calmly and professionally. He applies technical and interpersonal skill. He senses his own anger, frustration, fear, and anxiety but does not react to them.

The PM can always "cave-in" to the irrational demands of a powerful client or manager, but he does so without fear, and with the knowledge that he has done everything in his power to establish reason. The PM can also refuse the task and create a confrontation. Either way the Zen PM has done all that can be done to make the process work.

In either case, at the end of the negotiation there is an acceptance of the situation as it is. If the schedule is a pipedream that has been forced on everyone, the wise practitioner accepts that or opts out of the project. The in-between place, of taking on the project while being inwardly critical and resentful, is bound to create unnecessary tension and pain. It is a cop-out. By signing on for the journey, you implicitly agree to the terms of engagement.

As the project is performed, an effective manager controls the process and continuously informs stakeholders of progress and schedule and budget compliance. No matter what, the Zen PM operates fearlessly, knowing that the process is carrying the burden. Formal processes, like managing changes and issues, documenting the way the project unfolds, and assessing the results of its activities, provide a foundation for effective performance. Subtle communication and reliance on intuitive responses to moment-to-moment issues are used alongside of the more concrete approaches. Always there is a balance between extremes like analytical formality and intuitive, ad hoc behavior.

The process is fine tuned, moment to moment, adjusting for different conditions and people. Kaizen or Six Sigma or any formal ongoing improvement refines the process over time, both within a single project and across multiple projects.

At each step of the way, the Zen PM focuses on performance with concentrated discipline, moderated by moment to moment assessment and adaptation to the practical needs of the situation and each involved individual, including herself.

> **"Free yourself from mental slavery. None but ourselves can free our mind."**
>
> **Bob Marley,** *Redemption Songs*

Chapter 3
Managing Expectations: Goals, Objectives, and Project Success

Everyone has expectations. Attachment to unrealistic expectations is a root cause of suffering.

The key to managing expectations is to first acknowledge that people always expect something and then to consciously and explicitly find out what they expect.

Purpose

In *Alice in Wonderland,* Alice asks the Cheshire Cat which way to go at a fork in the road. In response, the cat asks her where she *wants* to go. When Alice responds that she doesn't know, the cat says "Well, then it doesn't matter, does it?"

In projects, goals and objectives set the stage, direction, and pace for the work. Success is achieving objectives and satisfying stakeholders' expectations. In this chapter we define what goals and objectives are and how to identify them in an iterative and interactive process between the providers and beneficiaries of project results.

Zen concentration and mindfulness are applied to listen to the voices of the customer, sponsor, and other stakeholders. The master PM understands the need for spending time and effort up front to make sure everyone is on the same page, even when everyone just wants to push ahead to "just get it done." The challenge is to balance the need to reach consensus on objectives with the need to stay open to the uncertainty that is almost certain to be operating during the early stages of the project and to achieve that balance without getting caught in "analysis paralysis."

Expectations are set regarding the project's results, schedule, and budget. But these are not all. Expectations also relate to the way the project will be carried out and the impact it will have on its environment.

Realistic expectations are based on the understanding that risk and uncertainty are givens, and that it is impossible to do the impossible.

> To work well in the world one must be skillful.
> Skillfulness combines realistic vision with the ability to actualize it.
> Skillfulness includes the ability to manage what in Zen are called the "afflictive emotions" such as anger, fear, greed and despair.

Goals and Objectives

Although no definitive definition of goals exists, we can say that *goals* are the overriding reasons for doing a project, while *objectives* are the more concrete, measurable results that come out of project performance.

Goals include reducing cost, eliminating errors, having a good time (as in planning an event). Objectives are expressed in terms of delivering a product or result ("the deliverable") that has a set of attributes (for example, behaviors, functions, dimensions, quality characteristics) within a certain time frame for a certain cost. For example, "In order to achieve our goal of reducing

costs while improving service, we will create a new way of processing the work that costs 25 percent less than the current way and delivers results in half the time."

Project requirements are the detailed descriptions of deliverables. *Deliverables* are the end products required to achieve the objectives. Requirements or specifications define the characteristics of the deliverables. For example, if the objective or goal of a project is to have a roomier, brighter, and more efficient kitchen, requirements will include the specific appliances, the exact size of a new window, the size of the island, and all the other details required to actualize the goal. The goal might be to make cooking more pleasant and effective.

Project success hinges on setting clear, mutually understood, measurable objectives. These must be a true reflection of the project's goals. In addition, sufficiently detailed requirements to direct the work of producing the right set of deliverables are needed. Objective-setting begins whenever the first idea or issue relating to the project's initiation emerges. Given the reality of change, objectives may be refined over the life of the project.

All projects must end. The end is reached when the client and sponsor accept the deliverables and agree that objectives have been met, or when the project is canceled. Clearly, well articulated objectives and requirements are needed to ensure that at the end there will be a way to objectively determine if the project has succeeded.

So What's the Problem?

> "Climate is what we expect, weather is what we get."
> Mark Twain[10]

Everyone knows this fundamental tenet of PM: Since projects are efforts to achieve objectives, make sure the objectives are known and accepted by the project stakeholders. It seems so simple. Just ask everyone what they want and give it to them. Ha!

Anyone who has worked on any project knows that even when people know what they want, they often have a hard time expressing it clearly and concisely. Often, people don't even know what they want. Sometimes, if you delivered what some people say they want, they would hate it.

Others know they want *something* but don't know exactly what it is. Sometimes you get a reasonably clear definition of what a person or group wants, but you then hear conflicting wants from others with equal or greater influence or need. And then there are those who just want what they want, when they want it, and for the price they want to pay. Their expectations may not match reality.

To make things even more difficult, many project outcomes are quite complex. People may have a good idea of what they want on the macro level (e.g., "We want a car."), but when it comes down to the specifics (e.g., "It must have four doors, six cylinders, emission controls that meet regulatory conditions, a sun roof, a GPS navigation system.") they get confused about what's important and what's just nice to have.

Setting expectations requires a communications process that is iterative and structured. This takes time and effort. In fact, setting the expectations for a project is often a project in and of itself.

So we know that objectives are necessary—that is PM 101.

The Zen Perspective—Inner and Outer Work

Earlier we defined the inner work as the effort you expend on your own self realization—perfecting yourself. The outer work is the effort you expend perfecting the form of your Zen arts. You use the outer work as a vehicle for the inner work.

Are you mindfully aware right now?

Remember Pat? As she becomes more and more able to get her clients to articulate what they wanted from her, validate that she got it right, and then pass on a clear action requirement to her staff, she found that in the more complex projects it took more than a single round of questions. As she found it necessary to get into detailed inquiry about objectives and requirements, she ran up against resistance. Her busy clients were just too busy and impatient to have a dialogue about what they considered to be trivial details. They expected Pat and her team to know what they wanted and to deliver it.

Pat knew from past experience that just delivering what she thought the client needed led to dissatisfaction and changes later in the project when the client finally got something, looked at it, and found it to be less than perfect.

When a particular client attempted to blow off her questions about his objectives and requirements, Pat found her frustration rising. She'd been practicing mindfulness for a while and was able to note the rising of her tension. She felt her anger. In the past she would have either "stuffed" her feelings or just disengaged from the conversation (she wasn't the kind of person to express her frustration to her clients) and taken the initiative to make up what she thought the client wanted.

This time she decided to handle the situation differently. She took a breath, felt her body against the chair, and noted the feelings she labeled as anger and frustration—the "afflictive emotions" most of us know. She took another breath and remembered that she was in the realm of relationships. Relationship, to the Zen practitioner, is a game to be played skillfully for the mutual benefit of all the players. All this took less than a minute. During that time she courageously accepted the need just to be silent, with her client on the phone.

> Try being silent for thirty seconds.
> Just follow your breath.
> How does it feel? Do you think your client can handle it?
> Can you handle it?

Then she said, calmly and authoritatively, "You know that if we don't spend a few minutes dealing with this now we will have to spend far more time later. We have been through this before. Let's try something different this time. Give me half an hour now or at a more convenient time in the next day or two so we can pin down your real needs."

Guess what! The client agreed to a meeting the next day, invited a knowledgeable colleague and they clarified the requirements amicably.

From the Zen perspective clarity is an essential element of successful living. When there is a lack of clarity one has a sense of uncertainty that manifests itself as a gnawing anxiety, sometimes very subtle and sometimes obvious. Mindfulness allows the PM to acknowledge the sense of anxiety quickly. Courage and right resolve enable the PM to take the time to promote clarity, even when faced with the pressure to "just get on with it."

Being Objective

Objectivity is the quality of having a basis in fact and/or logic. It is one of the most important tenets of Zen—seeing things as they are without being clouded by subjective beliefs, opinions, and conditionings.

Note the close relationship between the words *objective* and *objectivity*. In project management, objectivity hinges on the objectives of the project. Decisions regarding the approach to performing the project, for example, whether changes to requirements should or shouldn't be made, are based on the project's objectives. The objectives in turn are based on the project goals.

Again we are confronted with the need for balance. Finding the right balance between objectivity and the subjectivity of personal intuition is a challenge. Objectivity should be applied to every decision made in a project. At the same time it is necessary to recognize the power and importance of the subjective opinions of the stakeholders. The right balance between them cuts through the discord often associated with problem-solving and decision-making in projects.

In the Zen view, we accept the reality of subjective opinion. It is there, and it isn't likely to go away just because some theory says that objectivity is the way to go. As the practitioner matures, her objectivity enables clear seeing to differentiate objective, fact-based thinking from intuition.

Case Study—Cutting Through Opinion and Belief

Here is an example of how, by balancing objective and subjective views, the right project requirements can be identified and agreed upon.

On a project to re-engineer the commercial lending process in a global financial organization, there was a conflict about how much to automate the process of authorizing large loans to commercial borrowers. The technophiles knew that the whole process could be automated by creating an algorithm that would make a recommendation and then electronically pass the recommendation and the complex credit proposal prepared by the account officer to the desks of the senior executives, who were ultimately responsible for the decisions. The technophiles could show objectively that the solution was not only possible but that it would lead to a more efficient and cost-effective result. Efficiency and cost effectiveness were clearly a part of the stated project objectives.

Other stakeholders in the project were not so sure. They had a *feeling* that the kind of change being promoted would not be right. They couldn't quite put their finger on the real reason, but it had to do with cultural change and the way the organization operated at the highest levels. The technophiles considered these resistors to be Luddites[11] who feared change. Pushed by the technophiles and their numbers and facts, the other stakeholders had to better articulate their position.

As they explored it, they interviewed key account officers and senior executives and discovered two solid reasons for moderating the automation. One reason was that some of the most senior executives were computer illiterate and relied on their assistants and secretaries to act as intermediaries between them and the computers. The second reason was that there was a subtle training process that was taking place as the account officers made their presentations face to face to the seniors.

These issues when weighed against the efficiency and cost savings led to a change in objectives and requirements that ultimately saved the firm from a disruptive change process. In the longer term, the automation was enabled. It was phased in over a significant enough time frame to allow for the organizational change that would be needed to make it effective.

> **When goals and objectives become desires and drive unconscious behavior, we lose track of the big picture. We become reactive.**

How often do we become reactive, particularly in the face of negative emotions? In the process of communicating about expectations there are many opportunities to do the inner work that will take you a step further towards self perfection and make your outer work better. Each time impatience, fear, anxiety, or anger arises in response to some part of the work, can you note the feelings and be with them without reacting? These "afflictive" or negative emotions are self-generated. The same event on a good day is no big deal, but on a bad day it causes pain. Is the event causing the pain, or is it the quality of mind? Can you accept responsibility for your reactions? How in control are you of your own mind? How is being in control of your emotions—without stuffing or suppressing them—going to help in the outer work? The inner work?

Defining Objectives Iteratively and Realistically

The bottom line is: define objectives so that all project stakeholders (performers, clients, sponsor, etc.) have common realistic expectations. The result is a *written* statement of objectives that can be used as the reference point for all project evaluation, planning, and control. The objectives describe expectations. If the objectives have been well defined and communicated, there is a greater chance that conflicts will be avoided and expectations met.

> You can't see the big picture and the details all at once. Be realistic.
> Take multiple perspectives across time.

Objectives and requirements including the desired product, duration, and cost are best defined iteratively in layers of detail. As more is known, time and cost expectations are defined with increasing precision and refinement to make sure the triple constraints are fully aligned. The *triple constraints* are the three things the client and project sponsor are interested in: 1) a product and its value within 2) a schedule, or by a certain point in time, for 3) a cost that is within the budget.

Realistic expectations can be met within time and cost constraints. This depends on the availability and capability of people and their tools, facilities, and methods. But realistic expectations must also include the understanding that there is uncertainty: We don't always get what we expect, even when what we expect is realistic.

This is where wisdom comes in. An amazing number of projects are defined with unrealistic or "fuzzy" expectations. This is so because there is a complex relationship between the drive to fulfill the initial expectations of the most influential stakeholders and the time and effort needed to refine expectations so they are realistic and meet the needs of other, less influential stakeholders. Fear often drives this syndrome. The Zen project manager realizes that clarity and realism are fundamental to project success.

Take the case of a client who insists on the delivery of a complex product design within a few months. The client works with the sales rep of a design engineering firm, and together they come up with a fixed price and deadline but do not fully detail the exact nature of the design documentation or the specific needs that the product is to fulfill. These details will be figured out as the project proceeds. To make matters more complex, the client and sales rep do not take into consideration the fact that the design engineers are up to their limit with work for the next several months.

Because the project's deadline is so tight, there is little time to define requirements. The engineers expect that the client will be flexible and that they will be able to negotiate an acceptable design as the project proceeds. The client personnel feel that their company is paying a lot of money for the design and that they have the right to be quite demanding when it comes to quality. Because the engineers simply dove into the work, they are open to the risk of changes to the requirements later on in the project. But, because they expected that the client would be reasonable, they hadn't established a realistic change control process or set client expectations regarding the cost of changes. And because there is no clear statement of requirements, there is a strong likelihood that what the engineers view as changes will not be viewed as changes by the client. In short, there is a disaster in the making.

> **Strike the right balance between the useful drive to achieve and the obsession to control.**

The wise project manager, faced with the sales rep's deal with the client, would take the time to clarify expectations at the start. While the sale sets the conditions for disaster, it is the headlong dive into performance that actually creates the disaster. The wise project manager knows that taking the time to do the hard and often unappreciated work of clarifying expectations is a must. Fear and the impatient desire to "get moving" are observed and acknowledged, but <u>not</u> allowed to drive behavior. Note that to be truly wise, the PM must understand that saying no to the deal is an option.

How to Manage Expectations

Managing expectations is as much an art as a science. The art lies in realizing that expectations are subject to change based on exploration and negotiation. Managing expectations is a process of facilitating communications among people with divergent views on many aspects of the project.

The science lies in the recognition that best practices can be used to get mutually understood and accepted objectives and requirements.

The process begins with getting the parties to explicitly state their expectations. Since most project managers work on projects in a given area of expertise, they or the analysts on the team can ask the right questions to elicit stakeholder expectations. The basic questions boil down to "What do you expect, when, and for how much?" As the answer to the "what" question begins to be answered, the PM digs deeper: "What do you mean by a car? How many doors? How big an engine?"

As the answers come, follow-up questions dig even deeper, going into each aspect of the product in more detail to explicitly define each attribute. With the answers to these questions comes the ability to assess how realistic the time and cost expectations are.

To make this process easier and more effective, there are techniques that combine group workshops and graphical-based methods to identify, describe, document, and organize requirements in a structure that clearly aligns them with the objectives they fulfill.

Controlling Change

"We should find perfect existence through imperfect existence. The basic teaching ... is the teaching of transiency or change. That everything changes is the basic truth for each existence."[12]

One of the trickiest expectations involves change. Clients and project performers alike often expect that once they have stated the objectives and detailed them into requirements, they will *not* change their mind. This is a very unrealistic expectation; perhaps it is delusional. Always expect change. Change is a fact of life and a fact of project requirements.

Manage expectations by first getting everyone to at least acknowledge that there will inevitably be a desire for change. Then set up a change control process that enables positive change but inhibits other kinds of change. In this process, any desired change is described and evaluated with regard to its expected benefits and impact on costs, schedule, and risk.

A priority scheme is needed, otherwise everyone's desired changes become not just desires, but *must-haves*. One definition of a must-have is something that is needed to make sure the product will be fit for use and not harmful to its operators and users. For example, a change to a design to remove the danger of explosion and fire in a product would be a high priority change—one that should be made regardless of the impact on schedule or cost. Lesser priorities are assigned to changes that would improve product performance, reduce costs, or make the product look better. Decisions to proceed with any change are based on these priorities and the impact on cost and schedule vis-à-vis the benefits.

Often it is a best practice to postpone changes until after the product is delivered in its first version, unless there are safety considerations. Other changes can be postponed until a project is begun to upgrade or improve the product later in its life. This enables the original objectives to be met while recognizing the need for continuous improvement. As above, the decision to make a change now, postpone it, or reject it completely is based on a conscious weighing of benefits vs. costs on project life and product success.

Since change is inevitable, we not only implement the process to control it, but also allow budget and time to address authorized changes, and time and effort to decide which changes to authorize. A change reserve is standard operating procedure in some fields, like construction and engineering, but is ignored or even discouraged in others. Those who do not plan for change are almost guaranteed to suffer the consequences of unmet expectations: Schedules and budgets will <u>not</u> be met, and the product, while it may satisfy the letter of the requirements, may not satisfy the client and product users.

From the outset, it is necessary to highlight the reality of "potential variance." Potential variance is the possibility that there will be a difference between planned results and actual results. There is always potential variance.

The wise PM will give estimates in ranges and will explicitly define contingency plans and reserves to include uncertainty in the project plan. When uncertainty is accepted as a fact of life, then expectations are more likely to be realistic.

Remember, change is inevitable. Expect it. Plan for it. Manage it throughout the project's life and account for it when considering the life of the product.

Recap

The Zen approach is founded on practical realism. Unrealistic expectations are the root of unease and unease leads to conflict and a drain on energy that can be better expended to achieve positive results.

Managing expectations is a critical factor in successfully managing projects. In the end, the degree to which the expectations of clients and project sponsors are met is the measure of project success. Project goals and objectives drive project performance and are the material reflection of expectations. Make sure that these are acknowledged and accepted by all parties to the project. Elaborate them to create a well-organized statement of requirements, which are the project's detailed objectives. Use objectives and requirements as the basis for the acceptance of project results.

This promotes objectivity, and objectivity helps to remove the seeds of conflict and stress during project life.

As in all aspects of project management, the inner work is performed as the outer work gives rise to the feelings that cause us to react. We recognize that these feelings are self generated—not caused by the other guy or the situation but by our own attachments and conditioned responses. We learn to rest with these feelings, neither reacting nor denying them. Then we can think clearly and act appropriately.

The chapters on estimating risk and delivering quality results further explore managing expectations and offer fertile ground for the inner work.

Chapter 4

Estimating:
Pushing Back to Negotiate Realistic
Estimates and Schedules

Zen cuts through complexity to arrive at practical core principles.

Purpose

Estimates set expectations, and meeting them is a primary measure of project success.

Estimating is predicting the future. We estimate to determine project duration, effort, and cost; we estimate resource requirements, and we estimate when we schedule events. Of course, no one without special powers can predict the future with 100 percent accuracy, unless the prediction also includes the possibility of error.

In this chapter we explore the interplay between product, cost, and schedule and how to negotiate the trade-offs among factors that drive and influence estimates. We will discuss the critical concept of iterative estimate refinement in a "rolling wave" approach in the context of Zen. And we will address the consequences of either pushing back or not against unreasonable demands.

The goal of estimating is to establish realistic, yet challenging schedules and budgets to deliver real results. This requires:

- questioning to get common understanding of objectives and their priorities

- resistance to unrealistic or irrational schedules and budgets
- use of past experience as a basis for estimating
- resistance to premature, definitive estimates.

Are you mindfully aware of the moments when you drift off to explore some juicy thought and lose track of what you are reading?

Mindfulness and concentration are strengthened each time you become aware of being distracted and you bring yourself back to the chosen object of your attention. Make reading an exercise in mindfulness and concentration.

The Zen of Estimating

I once had a boss who used a tactic when someone told him that they couldn't hit a desired target. He'd say "Well if *you* can't do it, we'll find someone who can."

Here is a great opportunity to do some inner work. What feeling does that bring up in a person? Especially someone who needs the job or finds displeasing authority figures threatening? A Zen practitioner seeks to see clearly by overcoming fear and delusional thinking.

How does this relate to estimating and scheduling? Fear arises when powerful clients and sponsors ask the impossible and we are forced to be the bearer of the bad news. Everyone knows the bringer of bad tidings is often mistaken for the news itself. We need the courage of our convictions, along with skillful means, to overcome our fear that we'll displease others, or lose a project, or worse yet, be labeled as a weak link in the chain of our organization's performance.

Perfecting the Form

Then outer work is perfecting the form. One critical aspect of perfecting the form or process is to become one with your tools and embody the form. The form in martial arts is the formal set of steps that is practiced to train the body to respond seamlessly (so fast and smooth it seems like a reaction) with the right moves at the right time. The form is a dance. The practitioner doesn't do the form when applying the art—the form is a formal sequence of movements. Ad hoc response, specifically suited to the situation at hand is what is needed in the real-world. We perfect the form to be better able to perform.

Estimating data from past experience, software, collaboration, and expert judgment are the tools used in estimating. Imagine a skilled carpenter with lots of experience. Could she make a cabinet without tools? Of course it's not the same with estimating. An estimator with experience can create an expert-judgment-based estimate, but it is far less likely to be accurate than an estimate based on recorded past experience, using a scheduling and estimating program. The form is the complex balancing act that takes place between the client, sponsor, project contributors, and project manager to negotiate a realistic schedule and budget based on requirements, resources, and the work approach.

Estimating Is Challenging and Important

Realistic estimating is among the most challenging aspects of project planning. It is also among the most important.

> "I conceive that the great part of the miseries of mankind are brought upon them by false estimates they have made ... "
> Benjamin Franklin[13]

Anyone can make an estimate that promises to meet externally set time and cost constraints. It takes an expert to create an estimate that can be actualized.

If the estimate is not actualized, that is, if the schedule isn't met or the budget is overrun, clients and sponsors may not be satisfied. Accurate estimates require courage, skill, effort, and data—and a willingness to apply them to get a reasonable and realistic sense of the expected outcome.

Master project managers are aware of causes and effects. We seek root causes.

ESTIMATING TERMINOLOGY

Availability refers to the amount of time that people can spend performing work, or the degree that equipment, facilities, and materials can be used. (For example, a piece of equipment may be available for use on a project between April 1 and 15, but not before or after because it is scheduled for use on another project.)

Duration is the span of time required to accomplish something.

Effort refers to the amount of person-time expended to perform work.

Estimate is an approximation of the time, resources, and cost required for an activity.

Negotiating is the process of reaching agreement between parties. In the context of estimating, it is the process by which schedules and budgets are set. The goal of negotiating an estimate is to agree upon a realistic time and cost for the delivery of an agreed upon project result.

Project cost is the sum of effort times the rate(s) per unit of person time, plus the costs of facilities, equipment, materials, and overhead. The budget is the expected cost of the project, and the actual cost is the result of the project expenditures.

Project result refers to a new or changed product, system, or procedure, an event, or any combination of material deliverables. The term product will be used to represent any project result.

Pushback refers to resistance to requests or demands. Pushback may be from project managers to clients and project sponsors or from clients and sponsors to project managers. Pushback may also occur between project performers and managers, in both directions. Pushback is part of negotiating.

Realistic means capable of being actualized under real-world conditions.

Schedule is the timeline made up of the set of activities and events or milestones that define the duration.

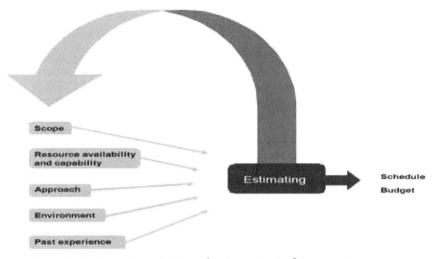

Figure 1: Estimating – A Complex Iterative Refinement Process

Study after study shows that the majority of projects finish "late" or "over budget." This often makes them failures in the eyes of key stakeholders. Estimates are a critical element in deciding whether or not to perform a project. Decision makers decide to proceed or not based on projected benefits, cost and time estimates, and on their understanding of the risk of not meeting expectations. Inaccurate estimates mislead decision makers and set the stage for project failures.

Attempting to meet impossible budget constraints or deadlines causes poor quality (people cut corners), burnout, interpersonal strife, and client relationship problems, including loss of credibility. Recently the CIO of a major global financial services company related how meeting a schedule by cutting down the time allocated for testing by two weeks cost the firm tens of millions of dollars, not counting the loss of clients and the ire of shareholders due to an avoidable technical error.

Quality shortfalls lead to problems throughout the life of the product, which is usually much longer than the life of the project. The cost of these problems far outweighs the perceived project cost savings promised by optimistic estimates.

Unrealistic estimates lead to burnout. Burnout leads to unnecessary turnover, often of the most valuable people, and to de-motivation of those who stay. Burnout is the result of well-intentioned people working above and beyond the call of duty to meet unrealistic expectations.

Interpersonal strife arises when finger pointing and blaming become a means for avoiding accountability for missed deadlines and over-budget results. Instead of seeking the causes of the problem in the estimating process, the fault is assigned to the project manager and other stakeholders. The project team disrespects leaders whom they view as delusional and perhaps even malevolent in their forcing of unrealistic deadlines and budget expectations. Internal groups and external suppliers also become the targets of blame for not meeting expectations that they never agreed to in the first place, or even if they had, were impossible to meet.

Client relationship and credibility problems are perhaps the most costly results of unrealistic estimating. They lead to loss of customers, outsourcing, and continuous conflict. Decisions to invest time, money, and resources in a project based on overly optimistic or pessimistic estimates lead to loss of opportunities for alternative investments that may have greater pay-offs. Chronically inaccurate estimating results in the loss of estimators' credibility. When people start multiplying estimates by fudge factors and then subtracting out the fudge, all semblance of rationality is lost.

Burnout, interpersonal strife, client relationship, and credibility problems are examples of PM suffering. In the Zen way, suffering is the result of clinging to desires that cannot be satisfied. By clinging to schedules and budgets that have no chance of being met, we create our own suffering. Effective estimates, on the other hand, promote increasingly greater trust among project participants. They set a bar that challenges project performers and urges them to excel. And they make future estimating easier by creating the data (recorded past experience) needed for future projects. Effective estimates remove a key source of conflict and stress. They promote thoughtful planning and decision-making.

Why do so many intelligent people create irrational plans that have little probability of being actualized? Based on informal surveys in courses and presentations, the most common reasons are: force from above ("My boss made me do it"), client demands ("If we didn't agree, they'd buy from someone else"), and wishful thinking ("Nothing will go wrong this time").

Failure to accept the fact that even the best estimates are just that, estimates, not actual results is a cause of suffering. Estimates do not determine the outcome (though they might influence it); they merely try to predict it.

In Zen, clinging is the root cause of suffering. Clinging is trying to hold on to things that cannot be held or trying to avoid the unavoidable. Clinging is the result of ignorance and delusional thinking. Delusional thinking is a common obstacle in project settings. It is a root cause of the estimating pains we have described. For example, some seem to believe that unrealistic schedules and budgets will get people to excel. Others act as if they believe that looking at risks and obstacles is counterproductive. Still others believe that estimating and scheduling are futile ("Since we never get it right, why bother?"). These beliefs—and others—must be questioned to reach clarity regarding estimating and scheduling.

Many people want estimates and schedules to be the result of a simplistic linear process. Just define scope and come up with a budget and schedule.

In reality, estimating is a complex, nonlinear process. First, as shown in figure 1, there is a negotiation process that includes a complex, priorities-based reevaluation of the factors of scope, resource assignments, approach, environment, and past experience. We start with objectives and requirements, there is an estimate; the estimate is too big. We negotiate to reduce scope (changing objectives and requirements) and/or to increase resources, and/or to change the way we will work. We assess the project for risks and uncertainties and fold in the results. We estimate again and again until we have an acceptable balance between scope, time, and cost. Then, as the project progresses and more is known about each of the factors that drive the estimate, the estimate is refined. There may be further negotiation every time the estimate is reevaluated based on greater knowledge.

Reactive behavior is another root cause of our estimating pains. Previously we referred to the afflictive emotions—fear, anger, frustration, among others. In estimating, the predominant afflictive emotions are fear and greed. Fear drives middle managers to set unrealistic deadlines and budgets and fear also drives their project managers to accept them. Greed is one of the drivers at the client and sponsor levels, where demands are made to drive the middle managers to drive their people.

Here is an example of where the inner work and outer work come together. The project manager uses the skill and knowledge of estimating principles and applies them in a practical and realistic way, given the circumstances. At the same time he is monitoring his own reactions, seeing fear and delusional thinking arising in his own mind and making the decision to let them subside before speaking and acting.

With courage and clarity, the Zen PM subtly questions, pushes back, and presents clear, concise, objective arguments along with reasonable alternatives. Of course the Zen PM knows that getting others to change their minds is no sure thing, regardless of the quality of the arguments or the clarity of the arguer. But, sometimes the cause and effect relationships will change and reason will reign. A key trick is to work with the impact of a poor estimate on the interests of the client and sponsor. Will it end up costing more, taking longer? What are the short and long term trades-offs? If there is no acknowledged pain from forcing overly aggressive or totally unrealistic time and cost objectives, then why would anyone change them? In the end, if irrationality reigns, it is up to the PM to make a choice—work with things as they are or say no to the project opportunity.

Effective Estimates

Certainly, there is uncertainty.

An estimate need not exactly hit the mark. An effective estimate is likely to be actualized within a stated range of possible outcomes. The size of the range depends on the degree of uncertainty about the estimate's driving forces. In estimating, uncertainty is certain. The diagram in figure 2 shows how we can get more realistic about estimating by recognizing that project success is determined by the degree to which the estimate predicts the outcome.

Success: Point or Cube?

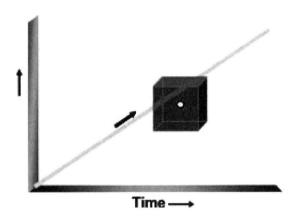

Time ⟶

Figure 2: Effective estimates come close to predicting the exact outcome[14]

Single point estimates imply certainty. The concept expressed in figure 2 above shows that there is uncertainty when it comes to estimating. Estimates predict the cost and time required to deliver some scope at level of quality. The cube represents a range of estimate accuracy. The more complexity, the more uncertainty, the bigger the cube.

Yet, many intelligent and well meaning people make and accept "single point estimates," which present a single value for cost and/or specific dates for completion and other project milestones. Single point estimates send the message that the estimate is predicting the precise outcome.

Clever project estimators present predictions in ranges and associate them with a probability of outcome. Clever clients and project sponsors expect, even demand, estimates that clearly communicate an accurate picture of the degree of uncertainty and the reason for it. We will discuss this in more depth in chapter 5 when we look at Risk.

Negotiate Rational/Realistic Estimates

It is not wanting that causes suffering. It is clinging to wants that cannot be met.

Projects start with a set of client and sponsor "wants". They might say, "We want a fancy widget by next Tuesday for $1.98."

The Buddha's First Noble Truth is the truth of suffering, or more accurately, the truth that we find ourselves in a situation that is unsatisfactory because we are faced with impermanence. Many people mistakenly believe that the Buddha's First Noble Truth means that suffering is caused by desire or wanting. They attempt to not want anything. But, in the Zen way, suffering is caused by clinging to wants that are impossible to satisfy; not to wanting itself. Wanting is normal, natural, and quite necessary in the real world of projects. Clinging is avoidable.

Anyone can make up a plan that makes it look as though the project will satisfy client and management wants. The trick is to create a plan that satisfies the business objectives that underpin the wants and can be actualized under real-world conditions.

Make use of past experience and assess the current situation to negotiate an estimate that is reasonable (it meets the needs of the situation) and realistic (it considers real-world conditions and uncertainty, and therefore can be actualized).

> **In Zen we see things objectively, unfiltered by what we want to see.**

Assessing and accounting for real-world conditions is a critical factor in creating a realistic estimate. These conditions include:

- the availability of resources
- scope change
- realism of delivery schedules
- time frames for permits and approvals
- testing and correcting defects
- the weather
- vacation schedules
- holidays
- labor disputes
- anything else that can influence the project's outcome

Negotiating the Constraints

The *triple constraints* are the three aspects of projects that most interest sponsors and clients: cost, results, and time to completion. These "wants" become constraints, project objectives and requirements. PMs constantly face the challenge of starting their projects with constraints that "do not compute." If they do not negotiate an effective resolution to this problem, everyone will suffer.

For example, a sponsor in a product development environment quite reasonably and cleverly insists on *fast, cheap, and good.* The PM is caught between that demand and the demands of his development team for either more time and money or the acceptance of lesser quality—that is, they can do *fast and cheap,* but not *good.* Clients and product managers often want speed and quality and are less concerned with project cost. They want *fast and good.* The sponsor, however, is concerned with project cost, but wants to satisfy the client as well. If time is of the essence to meet client or market needs, then the sponsor wants all three—fast, cheap, *and* good.

Conventional project managers say "pick two." Zen PMs know they can deliver all three, as long as the definitions of each are realistic. Instead of either-or thinking, we apply the principle of balance within continuums. In cases in which it is <u>not</u> possible to balance the three constraints, it is better to know in advance rather than find out late in the life of the project. Often it is better to not do the project and get nothing at all than to do the project and get late delivery of an inadequate product at even a reasonable cost.

It is the PM's job to strike the right balance among the needs of all the stakeholders—his own, the staff, the sponsor, the client, the product managers, regulators, and any others who may be affected by the project.

ESTIMATE DRIVERS

A project is a complex of interacting forces that can be expressed like an algebraic equation. The schedule and budget (the estimate) are a function of four variables: technique, resources, environment, and product.

Estimate Drivers

$$\text{Schedule \& Budget} = f(\text{Technique, Resources, Environment, and Product})$$

The **technique** is the process to be used in performing the project, including tools and methods.

The **resources** represent the full set of human and other resources, their capabilities, quality, and availability.

The **environment** consists of the surroundings within which the project will be performed, including the location(s) of participants, the working conditions, and culture.

The **product** represents the set of features, behaviors, and functions to be delivered by the project and includes geographical parameters such as whether it will be rolled out globally or used within a very limited area.

As in any equation, any change to one side requires a change in the other. If the schedule and budget are tightened, there will have to be some change in the variables.

Win-Win Solutions—Deliver Quality

The worst thing you can do is deliver substandard product, even if it is on time and within budget. The true measure of project success is whether the product meets the business need *and* delivers promised benefits. Substandard means that requirements have *not* been met and expected benefits *not* delivered. The measure of whether something is substandard or not is based on objective, measurable, and articulated criteria that include compliance with standards, requirements, and stated expectations. We'll look at this in greater depth in chapters 6, 7, and 8, where we discuss quality.

The second worst thing to do is to surprise the client or sponsor with a big bill or late delivery. Manage expectations.

Sometimes it is easier to satisfy the cost and time constraints by delivering poor quality. Being on time and in budget satisfies the sponsor (at least for the moment), satisfies the need of the delivery team, and often postpones the discovery of "failure" until after the end of the project. By that time, the project team is often long gone and no one is accountable. Software fails. Bridges collapse. Levees break. Buildings crumble.

All too frequently there is inadequate testing, often against inadequate quality criteria. Add to these conditions the absence of a strong "quality champion" and it becomes likely that the irresolute will take the easy way out and deliver on time and on budget at the expense of quality.

If you take a Zen view, trading off quality for time and cost is neither good nor bad. If the decision is made consciously, considering all alternative perspectives, then that's skillful. If the decision is unconsciously made without due diligence or driven by fear, then it is not skillful. Note that a skillfully made decision may also turn out to be a wrong decision in hindsight. Note also that a decision made consciously may be unethical. For example, a well-known auto manufacturer made a conscious decision to reduce costs by locating gas tanks on one of its models in a place that was guaranteed to increase the incidence of fires in collisions. They chose to save money and increase profits even at the cost of human life. In the end they failed because the cost of lawsuits, lost sales, and reengineering far outweighed the savings. The accountants and PMs were neither ethical nor skillful.

From a wisdom perspective, consciously doing something unethical is always unskillful. That is because the wisdom perspective integrates the inner work of self-actualization with the outer work of effective action towards desired results. On the inner level, in the Zen way, unethical behavior ultimately is unskillful. It creates a ripple effect that keeps the doer from becoming free of the barriers that obscure her underlying nature—clarity and emptiness manifesting as compassion in action.

So what does this have to do with estimating, you might ask. Well, how skillful and ethical is it to consciously underestimate a project to avoid the pressure from project sponsors and clients that comes from being honest about the real costs and time required to deliver a result? How skillful and ethical is it to underbid to "buy" a contract and then make up the cost differences by pricing changes that were fully anticipated by everyone but the unsuspecting client? How skillful and ethical is it to be totally honest and go out of business because everyone else underbids?

Conquer Fear—Push Back & Negotiate

Stephen Covey, in his book *The 8th Habit: From Effectiveness to Greatness,* reports on an interesting approach to what he labels "no deal" agreements, where the agreement is to "disagree agreeably." Called the doctrine of stubborn refusal, this approach comes from the armed forces:

"It means that when you know something is wrong and that it would result in serious consequences to the overall mission and values of the organization, then you should respectfully push back, no matter what your position or rank. You should speak up and declare yourself in opposition to the momentum of a growing decision that you are absolutely convinced is dead wrong. That's essentially living from your conscience—allowing your inner voice or light to guide your actions rather than giving in to the sway of peer pressure.

"It is important for people in high positions to officially endorse the doctrine of stubborn refusal. This legitimizes the right to push back, to call wrong wrong, and stupid stupid ."[15]

The project manager's job is to facilitate a plan that can be actualized without jeopardizing the quality of the result or the effectiveness of the organization. This implies confronting the powers that be with answers they may not like, pushing back, negotiating.

The power of the project manager or performer rests on the use of facts and logic. Remember Spock from *Star Trek?* Being a Vulcan, he had only the capacity to think logically. It is often best to emulate Spock and make sure you are relying on facts and logic. Respectfully ask questions like "Since it has consistently taken six months to do this kind of project, what makes you think we can do it this time in three?" in order to open the door to a rational dialogue or to establish that rational dialogue is impossible. In either case you, as the project manager, are on more solid ground.

Using a "facts only" style relies on taking an analytical approach to estimating, and documenting it in a way that can be understood by the sponsors, clients, and others who need to be convinced. Use a well-structured work breakdown structure that identifies all the work in levels of detail; document assumptions and risks, including resource availability and capability, the logical sequence of activities, and the nature of the product; provide trade-off options; and describe budget and schedule results clearly, in levels of detail that permit easy understanding of the big picture. You should also be able to drill down into the details to validate the big picture.

Objectives and Feasibility

How do you estimate? You start by getting stakeholders to agree that it is in everyone's best interest to have an effective (i.e., accurate and realistic) estimate. Next, make sure there are concrete, mutually understood objectives. Note the difference between objectives (wants) and estimates (probable outcomes). Concrete objectives say what is to be delivered, for how much, when, where and what at exactly what level of quality.

Then determine the degree to which meeting the objectives is likely, unlikely, or impossible. This means analyzing the expected conditions for the project. Will resources be available? Which ones? How long will it take to deliver supplies? How many times is the client likely to change his mind? How many errors will have to be fixed? …and so forth. The risk analysis is part of the estimating.

If it isn't likely or possible to meet objectives, say so. Push back. In the end you might still have the same constraints, but when the project has gone over budget or taken more time than expected, at least you will be able to "take the heat" more easily and the organization will be able to learn.

What does "taking the heat" mean? It means being able to withstand the penalties for *not* meeting the constraints. The Zen PM learns to let the fear of being fired or having his or her career ruined or being "yelled at" arise and be acknowledged. To be controlled by fear is like running a foot race with one hand tied to your ankle. The Zen PM can always take the heat, because the heat is just another condition that can be managed, along with all the other positive or negative thoughts, feelings, and events that come and go when managing a project.

But pushing back usually doesn't mean saying no; it generally means negotiating the right trades-offs to improve the probability of success.

> **Driven by wants alone, you choose the temporary pleasure of what feels good, at the expense of what is good. This is the wrong way to be "in the moment."**

What the client wants—the project's business objectives—drives the project. The client may want to improve profit margins or customer service, for example, or both. These objectives are achieved by delivering results—product, on time, and within budget. Part of the work of establishing the base for negotiating an effective estimate is questioning the objectives. You need to find out why it is important to get the widget by next Tuesday, and why is it a widget and not something else. You need to know why $1.98 is a constraint and how rigid the constraints are.

While it is true that estimates are negotiated by adjusting all the factors (resources, product, technique, and environment), the nature of the product and its ultimate use drive the project's time and cost, with resources, technique, and environment acting as influencing factors. Therefore, before estimating can begin in earnest, the project result (i.e., the product, process or event) must be defined, *to some degree.* What will be delivered to fulfill the objectives, to satisfy client wants? Product definition includes the identification of requirements, design (how the requirements will be met), delivery sequences, releases, quality attributes (e.g., how fast it must go, how long it must last under what conditions), acceptance criteria, and product lifecycle characteristics and constraints (e.g., how much will it cost to maintain the product.)

> The Zen mind is free from desire but enjoys the experience of wanting and uses it skillfully.
>
> In projects you must know what is wanted and why it is wanted before you can say how much it will cost and how long it will take to deliver.

Estimating involves questioning to understand the reason for the priority or strength of each objective, each product feature, or any other factor that may influence cost, time or resources. Sometimes the client's initial wants are whims—"Next Tuesday is the CEO's birthday and wouldn't it be nice to have the fancy widget by then?" Sometimes the wants are more aligned with business objectives: "Next Tuesday is the legal deadline for the project to be completed." Sometimes the wants are politically based: "We told the press that the widget will be available by Wednesday morning." By questioning the objectives and their strengths we can see where best to adjust the balance among time, cost, and product.

Strike a Balance

Pushback in the form of asking the right questions or making the right presentations stimulates negotiation. The negotiation enables project stakeholders to strike a rational balance among the constraints. What that balance point is depends on the situation. Sometimes the product features, functions, and quality should be reduced, sometimes the budget increased, and sometimes the schedule slipped.

Who decides? Well, ideally it is the decision team made up of the sponsor and client with the PM acting as facilitator.

But what if the decision team is incapacitated or momentarily irrational? Can the PM make the decision? This writer says "sure." Decide. Be as clear as possible about communicating the decision (remember, no surprises), and Just Do It. But remember the Law of Karma—every action has consequences. If you decide, then *you* must take responsibility for the result, and that may mean anything from a pat on the back to being fired, sued, or worse.

When faced with a decision to deliver poor quality in order to meet an irrational schedule, remember the 'O' ring from Challenger; remember pick-up trucks with exploding gas tanks; remember bridges that have fallen down and companies that have lost their reputation and market share because PMs delivered what the contract said was required on time and within budget but failed to satisfy the "real" need. With these in mind, moderate your fear with your sense of what's right and decide.

The Zen approach is about balancing *ethics,* quality, time, and cost to deliver excellence at the right price in the right time frame. Sometimes, as a last resort, that means bending the rules. Bending the rules means overcoming fear and behaving responsibly.

> **It is better not to agree than to agree with what you know to be wrong.**

Before you go and break the rules, estimate well, and work to make sure that everyone has the opportunity to appreciate the facts and logic of the situation. If you are going to push back against irrational demands and negotiate rational estimates, come to the table well prepared. The only real leverage you have comes from facts and logic.

> **Past performance is no guarantee of future performance, but the past is the best starting point for predicting the future.**

The Facts: History Repeats Itself—to a Degree_

A foundation of effective estimating, along with commonly understood objectives and a realistic assessment of expected conditions, is past experience. Estimates are most likely to be accurate if they are based on relevant past experience. If the projects you do are fairly repetitive— say you are renovating kitchen after kitchen, installing the same software application over and over again, or putting on a wedding every week—then make sure there is a historical record of the time, cost, and conditions for the projects you have done and use it to estimate future projects. Take into consideration similarities and differences between past and future projects. Everyone I run into knows this. Few do it.

Effective estimating rests upon a 'database' of past project performance. Ideally, this database is in a concrete form, perhaps electronically recorded and retrievable based on project descriptions or characteristics. But even if you are not that organized, you or someone you can consult has a project "database" in their head. Use it, but remember to factor in uncertainty and differences as well as memory lapses that skew the data (we tend to remember really good things best and suppress the really horrible stuff).

The goal is to look for projects that are most similar to the one you are estimating. When you find them, identify the potential differences and estimate how they will affect the outcome. Also identify the variance in outcomes among past projects, and make sure you are aware of the reasons for them, for example, differences between capabilities of performers, the degree to which the client changed his mind, or the season during which the project took place. Consider the causes of variation as you estimate.

With past experience as a base, it is far easier to convince others of the probable outcome. Without past experience, the opinion of the most powerful will prevail.

Iterative Estimate Refinement— the Rolling Wave Approach

> Few things are truly linear by nature. Life unfolds in a series of concentric circles.

Effective estimating rests upon the definition of objectives, requirements, designs, the conditions under which the project will be performed, and past experience. So, it would seem to follow that there is a simple sequence—define objectives, requirements, design, and conditions, then estimate. But as we have said, real life is not so simple.

Generally, clients and sponsors want to know how much a product will cost and how long it will take to deliver before the product is fully defined, resource availability is known, and other factors can be assessed. Since cost and duration are primarily driven by the product's requirements and design, a premature desire for a definitive estimate can be a big problem.

To satisfy needs for quick or early estimates, we rely on the "rolling wave" approach. In this approach, an initial estimate is given for the whole project but with a broad range of variance that recognizes the degree of uncertainty regarding scope, resources and other factors. This provides high and low estimate boundaries. At the same time a more definitive short range estimate is given for the next set of work needed to create a more definitive estimate with a much narrower range of variance. Depending on the project size among other criteria there can be subsequent long and short range estimates provided at checkpoints during the project.

The initial estimate gives the client/sponsor a sense of how much time and cost must be expended before having a better estimate upon which to base a decision to continue the work or not. It also gives a sense of the worst, best, and most likely outcomes upon which to decide whether to invest in further work or not.

> **Acknowledge uncertainty, while making use of your experience and expertise to minimize it.**

Effective, early, high-level estimates are made so that the definitive estimate is within range of the high to low estimates set initially. These top down estimates are made by looking at the project as a whole and are based on analogy with similar projects, or by using algorithms (formulas based on past experience). The alternative, "bottom up" estimates are based on the analysis of the project's activities, their sequence, effort requirements, and other characteristics. These are made later in the project when there is sufficient knowledge.

Bottom up estimates tend to be more definitive than the early top down estimates. Any differences between top down and bottom up estimates should be reconciled to make sure that assumptions are valid and the estimating is as accurate as possible.

In very large projects there may be several points in the project life at which more definitive estimates are given. In long projects, it is wise to regularly reassess the estimate to completion based on the current project objectives and conditions.

Getting the Right Estimates from Contributors

Projects are performed by people who contribute their efforts. Each contributor should be expected to offer estimates of his or her work, or to validate the estimates of the work made by others.

This "should" is a best practice that helps to get buy in for the estimate. The more the performer is bought into the estimate, the more likely it is that the estimate will be met. People feel comfortable being accountable for performance criteria (i.e., meeting deadlines and budgets) that they have had a say in creating. The practice also leads to more accurate estimates and to a training of the contributors in project management practices. Everyone is managing projects or sub-projects (even activities performed by individuals are mini-projects given that a project is "a temporary endeavor undertaken to create a unique product, service or result"[16]).

As the recipient of an estimate from any contributor, at any level in the project, it is wise to ask the following questions:

- What assumptions have you made about the amount of dedicated time you will spend, the deliverable and the way it will be evaluated and accepted, the availability and nature of resources, and the way you will approach the work?

- What inputs do you need before you can start and/or finish the work, and when will you need them?
- What is the worst case scenario and how much time and effort will the work take if it comes to pass? How probable is it? What can you do to avoid it or mitigate its impact?
- What is the most likely scenario and estimate? What makes you think it is most likely? Under what conditions will it come to pass?
- What is the best-case scenario and estimate? How probable is that? What can you do to make it more likely?

Recap

Estimate realistically and rationally.

Project success depends on realistic expectations. If expectations are met, project stakeholders are satisfied and the project can be deemed successful. Effective estimates set realistic expectations that can be met.

Effective estimates rest on: the ability to negotiate by overcoming the fear of pushing back against irrational demands for unrealistic schedules and budgets; relevant past experience and a logical and analytical approach that considers risk and uncertainty; the availability and capability of resources; the nature of the product; the approach to be taken to perform the project; and the project's environment.

Estimating includes asking the right questions to clearly and concretely define project wants, objectives, and detailed requirements. It seeks to negotiate realistic estimates to factor in all of the estimate drivers and presents them as ranges based on an assessment of uncertainty. Effective estimates are refined as increased knowledge of project requirements and conditions becomes available.

From the Zen perspective, the principles that are applied are courage, realism, and a balance that combines intuition and concrete, analytical estimating based on concrete facts from past experience. Clinging to what cannot be achieved is the cause of suffering. As a PM you can cut through your own clinging and make it easier for others in and around your project either to not cling or at least to cling to expectations that have a high probability of being met.

Chapter 5
Avoiding Risk-Management Avoidance

> **If you look only at what you want to happen, you are less likely to bring it about.**

"Judge, I have to be frank. The biggest problem I have in this whole situation is getting you to take it seriously. Even if it is 1 in 10 that I am right, you can't act as if the chances are zero. Can you maybe ask yourself if you're in denial?" Scott Trurow[17]

When I read this quote it struck a cord. There are people involved in project work who behave as if there was certainty regarding various issues. The attorney asks the judge if he has actually considered the possibility that what he believes to be 100% correct is possibly incorrect. How often are we faced with people who, like Trurow's judge, treat the uncertain as certain? Are they in denial or are they using denial as a tactic?

Purpose

Fear often arises in the context of estimating. It arises because there is uncertainty about the estimate and about the way the estimate and its accuracy will be received. Will the client, sponsor or his boss face the estimator with denial and disapproval? Will the estimator be blamed for the estimate inaccuracy? Will there be forgiveness?

As with any emotion, the Zen practitioner observes its arising, allows the feelings to take their course, sees them for what they are: a complex of thoughts and feelings that manifests as physical sensations. If possible, the practitioner does not react. She observes, perhaps she analyzes the cause of the fear, she assesses options and responds in a way that is perfect for the situation. All this occurs in the split seconds of real time.

In managing expectations and estimating, uncertainty is a critical issue. Expectations are not just about clarity regarding what will be delivered, when, and for how much. Expectations are also about how "firm" or certain those expectations are. Everyone expects delivery by the schedule end date, but do they expect it with 100 percent certainty? If so, they may be disappointed. As we pointed out in the previous chapter, success criteria are best expressed in terms of ranges and the probability of hitting inside or outside the range.

This is where risk management comes into play—when planners and other stakeholders look at the "dark side" and confront uncertainty. Everyone knows, intuitively, that uncertainty is the only certainty, but often people act as if they have forgotten. In this chapter, we will explore what risk management is, how and why people avoid addressing risk and uncertainty, and how to counter that avoidance. We will explore the interplay between the outer work of risk assessment, planning, and control and the inner work of working with intuition, emotions like fear, and objective, rational thinking.

> "Investigate something to see its benefit or harm, examine whether it is appropriate and suitable or not; then after that you can carry it out."
> **True Record of Sushan**[18]

Risk is uncertainty about positive and negative events, benefits, and harms. In the Zen way, the goal is to see things as they are. Assessing risk, candidly and formally, brings reality into focus and allows project planners to promote positive events and minimize the occurrence and impact of negative ones. While it is logical and effective to look at decisions from as many perspectives as possible, we often find people who avoid looking at them from the dark side, sometimes out of a fear of appearing negative.

Risk Management Avoidance

> "Denial is a common tactic that substitutes deliberate ignorance for thoughtful planning. "
>
> Charles Tremper[19]

Risk management avoidance is the tendency to ignore risk—refusing to acknowledge the possibility of negative events and then not spending time and effort to identify, analyze, and plan for them. Perhaps it is an attempt to deny the reality that we are not in complete control and are subject to uncertainty.

When risk is ignored in project initiation and planning, the result is unrealistic expectations and the ripple effects that result from them. Ripple effects include schedule and/or budget overruns, benefits shortfalls, quality shortfalls, and disharmony among the stakeholders. When risk is ignored, the project team loses the opportunity to avoid or mitigate risks. Ignoring risk promotes reactivity. Risk management, on the other hand, supports a proactive approach.

Risk avoidance is the tendency to avoid situations that may involve loss or failure or in which there is significant uncertainty. While risk avoidance *may be* a problem because it can lead to missed opportunities based on emotional rather than analytical motivation, it is understandable. *Risk management avoidance is always a problem.*

In fact, from the Zen perspective, avoidance, in the sense of not looking at something that is clearly present, is a real problem. It is a sign that objectivity has been lost to an attempt to block out some inconvenient or undesirable reality. Of course once we accept the reality of risk, avoiding it is an excellent strategy.

The Zen PM seeks to see things as they are, avoid conditioned responses, and be as realistic as possible. Being realistic means acknowledging positive and negative possibilities as well as the inevitable uncertainty involved in any complex effort performed over time. Give up aversion to negative events and the attraction to positive ones to enable an unbiased assessment of what *might* happen.

Risk management avoidance is linked to the idea that those who bring up negative risks are enemies, pessimists, and/or defeatists. Project proponents are eager to convince sponsors and clients to authorize their projects. For these proponents, risk analysis gets in the way. An idea, whether it's to launch a product or a war, is harder to sell if the uncertainty of expected returns is highlighted. In this case, risk assessment is avoided in a conscious effort to misinform decision makers.

In other cases, project and product champions may think that their concepts are perfect. Therefore, risk assessment would simply be a waste of time.

Throughout history political leaders, military leaders, senior executives and many others have purposely or mindlessly ignored risk and plunged into disastrous actions without being prepared for the consequences. The annals of military history, in particular, are filled with examples of this behavior.

Look at any military or commercial disaster and ask what differences would a fully objective risk assessment and rational decision-making and planning have made? How many lives might it have saved? How much money?

Of course there are also those who are planning-averse and tend to think the only way to operate is to handle things as they come up in the natural flow of events. They too see risk assessment, like the rest of planning, as a waste of time; a depressing one at that.

At a professional services firm, risk assessment is inhibited because sales people, their clients, and senior managers dislike uncertainty. They want single-point estimates and guarantees. They avoid risk assessment because it breaks into their illusion that things can be certain.

In other situations, people feel that talking about or, worse yet, describing and writing down negative events will magically bring them on.

> Are you awake?
> Mindful of where your thoughts have taken you?
> Is your concentration strong enough to help you stay with the point of attention you have chosen?
> Sense the body, the breath. Breathe in this present moment.
> Read on.

Overcoming Risk Management Avoidance

So, how do we overcome risk management avoidance? How do we to get people to see things as they might really be?

The answer is simple, though not necessarily easy: Accept the reality of uncertainty, and then use effective risk management techniques to assess and address it. This boils down to a disciplined effort to overcome delusional thinking.

> Thinking about the negative is not negative thinking.

Changing is hard. It usually begins with highlighting the "pains" caused by unrealistic expectations. Raise the uncomfortable subject of past failures and chronic problems. If people are unwilling to hear about them, maybe they are not ready for change, and you need to accept that; some say a person or organization must "hit bottom" before it is ready to change. In the wisdom traditions, we say that there must be an 'opening'—some experience that makes it no longer possible to be in unconscious avoidance. We see and accept our condition. Without motivation, there is neither voluntary nor managed change. One of the greatest motivators is pain. We are reminded of the painful result of General George A. Custer's failure to assess risk: he and all of his men were killed.

Once there is an awareness of the connection between chronic problems and risk management, the next step is to get people to acknowledge two key principles:

1. Uncertainty is a certainty.

2. Identifying and analyzing risk does *not* magically increase the probability of its occurrence. In fact, identifying risk actually enables planners to avoid or reduce the probability and/or impact of negative risk events.

Pat's Risk Experience

Remember our friend Pat? She continues her play with the Zen project management approach. Her group's performance and her client's avoidance of chronic issues have buffered the clients from the reality of the situation and of the possibilities of more effective performance.

Pat recognized the need for constant reality checks when taking on new work and bringing them up in a "Spock-like" way. Spock didn't hold back on anything that was logical. He had no understanding, no experience of the right side of the logic/intuitive-emotional dichotomy. He was purely analytical.

Pat simply began asking questions like, "Are you aware that if we commit to that date and miss it we might really upset our external clients?" She began saying things like, "There is a high risk that we will encounter quality problems after we deliver the project results if we cut corners now."

At first it felt strange to be the only person raising these issues. She felt fear and anxiety based on thoughts that she might be rejected and penalized for not just saying, "Yes, we'll do it." She watched her feelings. She decided to allow the discomfort they manifested in her body and "go for it." At first she had to play at being firm and confident. Over time it became natural. The negative feelings weakened and in time disappeared.

Multiple Perspectives

Among the ways to get people to get past their avoidance is Edward DeBono's Six Thinking Hats (Edward de Bono, Six Thinking Hats, MICA Management Resources, Inc., 1999) approach. DeBono's process has problem solvers look at problems and solutions from six perspectives.

- *White Hat:* Focus on the data available to gain an analytical, fact-based perspective.
- *Red Hat:* Look at the problem using intuition, gut reaction, and emotion.
- *Black Hat:* Look at all the bad points of the possible solutions. Look cautiously and defensively. Try to see why something might not work.
- *Yellow Hat:* Adopt the optimistic viewpoint that helps you to see all the benefits of the possible solutions and the value in them.
- *Green Hat:* Creatively brainstorm out-of-the box solutions.
- *Blue Hat:* Engage in process control by looking not at the specific content of the problem but at *how* you are addressing it.

The thinking behind the Six Hats approach, and others like it, is that you can't be effective in decision-making unless you take all perspectives. Within this model, the Black Hat perspective represents risk management. The model makes this more palatable to those who are risk-management-resistant by regarding risk as just one of the multiple views required for effective planning and problem solving. Sell this idea to the most senior members of your organization and they will make sure the ones selling them ideas for projects bring the full picture into focus.

Black Hat thinking about the negatives highlights the weak points in a solution. It allows them to be eliminated, altered, or overcome through contingency plans. This kind of thinking helps to make solutions tougher and more resilient. It can also help you to spot fatal flaws and risks before you embark on a course of action. Black Hat thinking about the negatives is "forced" because many successful people get used to thinking positively and cannot see problems in advance. Black hat thinking and planning for the negatives prepares them for difficulties.

Note that we are focusing here on Black Hat thinking, the negatives, the dark side of future possibilities, because we are dealing with risk. Don't overdo it. Getting too pessimistic is just as unskillful as not being pessimistic enough. Skillful planning is all about striking the right balance among all perspectives. This is another wisdom principle that keeps coming up over and over again—balance all the forces to achieve a dynamic and effective forward-moving momentum.

The Risk Management Process

By taking a Blue Hat (process) perspective, in which we clearly connect the ability to succeed with the way we work, we are more likely to bring people to effectively manage risk. The risk management process according to Project Management Institute's *PMBOK® Guide,* 3rd edition, is:

1. Risk Management Planning: How will we manage risk?
2. Risk Identification: What are the possible risks?
3. Qualitative Risk Analysis: What are the probability and impact (subjectively)?
4. Quantitative Risk Analysis: What are the probability and impact (statistically)?
5. Risk Response Planning: What can and should we do about the risks?
6. Risk Monitoring and Control: What is going on in terms of risk event appearance and the application of responses?

At first glance this is a daunting process. Six steps. Complicated terminology. Probability and quantification. Yikes!

Boiling it down, we find that the process is to decide how you'll manage risk, assess the risk, figure out what you'll do about it, and then do it when and if you have to. "Well that's just common sense and good practice," you might be thinking. "What's Zen about that?" Nothing and everything. Zen is nothing special. It is being naturally, objective.

Risk management planning is a critical element. It is the step where the buy-in for performing risk management is obtained, roles and responsibilities are identified, and the process is tailored to the needs of the project. It is a best practice to have a consistent approach to risk management across many projects, if not the entire organization. It is wise to make sure there is sufficient flexibility to enable that process to be adapted to the needs of each project.

Here again we have common sense and best practices. What is more natural than adapting a principle to the needs of the situation in which it is to be applied? The master craftsperson doesn't use a sledgehammer to drive a peg into a fine piece of furniture. The PM practitioner who seeks to master the art uses the right tools for the job.

Like any aspect of project management, risk management has to be scaled to the needs of each project. Risk management need not be too complex or require a statistician or sophisticated tools. Depending on project size and complexity and on the capability of the organization, risk management can be done across a broad spectrum of levels of precision and complexity. This continuum ranges from simple brainstorming and subjectively based analysis to the use of sophisticated quantitative and statistical risk management tools like Monte Carlo analysis (an approach that involves simulating a project to statistically assess the probability of different possible outcomes).

> **Managing risk is critical.** *How* **you manage risk is based on the needs of the situation.**

Assessing risk means identification and analysis. *Risk identification* names what can occur and can be as simple as brainstorming likely risks. However, it is far more effective to use risk checklists, based on past experience. Most risks are known. They have occurred before in similar circumstances. We can know them through anecdotal evidence, informally, or through more formal, statistically valid evidence. Either way, the kinds of things that can happen are predictable based on past experience. That is the basis for effective planning. It is where lessons learned through the analysis of past performance meets planning and risk management.

Risk analysis, qualitative and/or quantitative, is performed to iden-tify the probability of occurrence and impact of risks so as to prioritize them and analyze them for their effect on the project as a whole. The project manager scales the technique to the needs of the project. For example, if the project is to put on an event like a wedding or holiday party, performing a statistically correct analysis using expensive and complex computer-based simulations is probably overkill. For a project to build a cruise ship or dig a tunnel in a city like Boston, the time and expense of a quantitative analysis using computer based statistical tools is clearly warranted.

Response planning, monitoring, and control are summed up as *handling the risk.* This is where the payoff comes for doing the assess-ment. Once we have identified and analyzed risk, it is then possible to decide consciously on how best to address and monitor it during the project's life.

As an example of informal risk management, my wife and I wanted to use the showers and toilets in our coop's gym locker rooms while we renovated our bathrooms. However, the gym facility was also being renovated, with a scheduled completion date of October.

We did a simple analysis. *Probability:* nothing in our building ever happened on schedule, and this renovation was large and complex. Further, progress reports and estimates to completion were wishful thinking. *Impact:* If the locker rooms were not completed we would find it rather difficult to live in Manhattan without indoor plumbing. *Decision:* While we wanted to get moving on our bathrooms, we decided to wait until the locker rooms were actually functional; and we were happy: The locker room renovation was six months late.

This example also brings out the need to assess risk across multiple projects, considering the entire environment. What is going on in and around your project? What has happened in the past? How likely is it to happen again? How could it affect your project? Is it worth doing something about it? What?

Risk Management Is Iterative

Since risk management is a part of estimating, it is iteratively performed across a project's life. It begins with a preliminary or high level assessment, coupled with making decisions and developing responses that can avoid or mitigate risks.

Preliminary risk assessment takes a high-level view. It is part of the first or early waves in rolling wave planning. Rolling wave planning refers to the approach in which estimates and plans are made and refined at various stages of a project. As more is known in greater detail regarding project objectives, resources, and other factors, the more likely it is for the estimate and plan to be accurate.

As an example, early assessment might identify a high probability risk that the sources of requirements (such as product users, sponsors and support people) won't be available during detailed requirements definition or that a particular design will require knowledge *not* available in the project organization. These realizations become the impetus for getting the sponsor and client to assign dedicated and knowledgeable people for requirements definition and for the decision to either avoid the design option or mitigate the risk by training or arranging for external assistance.

Detailed risk analysis is part of detailed estimating. Detailed estimating is based on a more refined definition of the project and the product and is associated with the later waves of rolling wave planning. The more detail, the narrower the range of probable outcomes. The more detail, the more the risks relate to individual activities.

Risk assessment leads to the identification of reserves and multipoint (e.g., pessimistic, most likely, and optimistic) estimates and schedules. These are used to set expectations and enable effective decision-making. The reserves and the range of expected outcomes are the direct result of risk management. Expressing all estimates in terms of the range of probable outcomes and their probability of occurrence is the surest way of communicating the uncertainty that is present in projects at various points in their life.

Recap

Our goal is to ensure that expectations are realistic. Risk is a given. Addressing risk consciously is a critical ingredient to effective project planning and performance. There is a tendency in some organizations' settings to avoid addressing risk, often because there is a fear of facing negative possibilities and acknowledging the degree of uncertainty. Avoidance is often unconscious but may also arise from the desire to promote some project by making it seem more attractive than it actually is.

Failure to take a well thought out risk management approach, performed across project life and as an integral part of planning and estimating promotes poor decisions, surprises, and reactivity—knee-jerk responses that often make things worse. Further, planners who avoid risk management lose the opportunity to squeeze unnecessary risk out of their projects by proactively avoiding or mitigating it.

Effective risk management is performed in the context of the progressive elaboration of project scope and rolling wave (i.e., iterative refinement) estimating. The wise project manager makes sure that expectations are managed and that the payoff from taking a realistic view of the future is acknowledged by everyone, and especially the most powerful players in the game. This means that the senior players, the ones who make the big decisions and motivate everyone else, understand the bottom-line effects of ignoring possibilities that may impact projects.

All this technical PM risk management stuff is standard, widely accepted best practice. "Everyone knows it," you might be thinking. Few believe that they can predict the future with a 100 percent accuracy. So why go on about it in a book on Zen? Because, while we may understand something intellectually, it does not guarantee that we will apply it. When we know something to be right and we do not apply it, feelings arise. What are they for you? Frustration? Self-blaming? Guilt? Embarrassment? Maybe nothing?

In the wisdom way, we do not want it to be normal to know what it means to do something the right way and then do something else. We want to make conscious and skillful choices. When we do not follow best practices like rational risk analysis, we can watch the feelings, see where they arise from, and learn more about ourselves. We can renew our resolve to use every experience as a means for self-actualization. Again, we have the interplay between the perfection of the form—the outer work—and the perfection of self—the inner work. And, it is all managed playfully; joyfully.

We have used the word "work" a lot—inner work, outer work, and working on yourself.

Zen is a joyous way. The first sign of awakening is joyfulness; joyfulness that comes from seeing things as they are, seeing our delusions, resting in our natural state. We play. We "whistle while we work." Playing means being open to whatever happens; ready to adapt, unconstrained by a fixed idea of the outcome.

I remember a time in Kyoto, Japan visiting a Zen temple with a few other Westerners. We were greeted by a monk holding a cardboard TV screen up in front of his face. The center was cut out and he was speaking to us from this cardboard TV. He was beaming. Joyfully he explained to us that he always wanted to be a TV star and now he was one.

ARE YOU MINDFULLY AWARE?

Each time you realize that you are *not* mindfully attending to the present is a moment of awakening.

Then there is the possibility of conscious choice about the next thing to attend to.

Thoughts arise. If they are interesting, we give them our attention and a chain of thoughts forms. This chain of thoughts takes our attention off on a little trip. It can be a pleasant one or not, but is engaging. Have you had this experience? What happens when you realize that you are off on a mind trip? Do you have the discipline and concentrative power to let go of that thought chain and bring your attention to one you choose consciously? This shifting from thought chain to thought chain is like changing channels on the TV. If the current program is engaging, it is hard work to let go of your attachment to it and move to the next channel.

Chapter 6
Delivering Quality Results

> Quality results require a quality process founded on the principles of clarity, realism, right balance, and acceptance that uncertainty is the only certainty.

Purpose

So far we've looked at the big picture of managing expectations, then at estimating and risk management. In this chapter we explore the challenge of arriving at a common definition of what is to be delivered—the expected results, be they products, events or other deliverables. Quality is measured in terms of the degree to which the product or other results satisfy the client's needs. Alternatively, it is defined as fitness for use or compliance to specifications. A main point in project management is to define the criteria that the result will be measured against as precisely and completely as possible to enable stakeholders to objectively evaluate quality, as far as that is possible. This definition is stated in a requirements document or specification that addresses features, functions and behaviors.

Projects are performed for results; they are a means to an end. Of the three major project objectives—results, time, and cost, *results* is far and away the most critical. Note that we are using the word "results" here instead of product or quality.

Even though time or cost may be very important to the project's outcome, success ultimately requires delivering the results wanted by those who put up the money and resources for the project. Results that satisfy expectations are made possible by agreeing upon mutually understood, relatively stable objectives and the requirements and specifications that describe them in detail.

In this chapter we address the need to make "quality" objectively measurable, without forgetting the need for subjective assessment. There are degrees of "goodness" and a balance among results, cost, and time. We discuss the critical need for quality control to make sure, before it is delivered, that what is delivered meets expectations. Just as we achieve success by managing expectations in effective estimating and risk management, we will also rely on managing expectations to arrive at a mutually understood definition of *quality* among all parties to the project. Defining quality is the key to ensuring that we can deliver it. Of course, defining quality is no easy task.

The Zen Perspective

> The Zen perspective seeks balance among "seemingly" contradictory factors, like subjectivity and objectivity. Continuums abound. Stop 'either/or' thinking.

Balance and paradox are critical elements in the wisdom tradition. The tendency of many to separate opposing concepts like objectivity and subjectivity is replaced by the recognition that they are elements in a unified whole. Both coexist in a continuum from total objectivity to total subjectivity. Between the extremes are infinite points at which the two are present with various degrees of predominance—a little subjectivity with a lot of objectivity, and so forth.

Life would be easy for project managers and performers if measurable, objective quality criteria were fully articulated from the very beginning of a project. However, it appears to be that the harder we try to "manage by the numbers," the more we are faced with the reality that complexity and human nature get in the way. The right balance between subjective and objective perspectives is critical to success.

The Zen PM approach counsels us to enter the process with eyes wide open, test all assumptions, and rely on open communications, committed to writing, in order to establish realistic understandings among clients, sponsors, and the people who serve their needs.

To set up the conditions that will lead to an optimum outcome for the project, precisely define what can be defined and clearly and precisely identify what cannot, in objective terms. Use common sense and intuition along with analysis to identify to the client the real requirements and their priorities. Highlight the unknowns and uncertainties.

Terminology

Many terms are used when referring to the complex of product, results, and quality. We will use the term *results* to mean the complete impact of the project. This includes the product itself. It also includes the benefits and/or negative impact the product has on the world. The *product* is the direct output from the project—for example, the house, the computer system, the event. Impact from the product's use is where the real pay-off is.

Quality is far more difficult to define. The dictionary definitions include 1) an essential property, 2) character or nature, 3) grade, degree of excellence. In the project management and quality management realms, quality is commonly defined as the degree to which a result satisfies expectations and is fit for use. That is how we will use it here.

The trickiest part of quality is satisfying expectations. Expectations are the thoughts people have about the outcome—what they envision. In order to minimize confusion and reduce the risk of leaving people dissatisfied, effective project managers take the time and effort to make sure that expectations are clearly known. This is the outer work that involves patient persistence to go through a disciplined process to describe expectations as requirements and specifications. As the outer work is done, the practitioner confronts the personal barriers to doing the inner work.

> "Quality. . . you know what it is, yet you don't know what it is."
> ... Some things are better than others, that is, they have more quality.
> But when you try to say what the quality is, apart from the things that have it, it all goes poof! ...
> But if you can't say what Quality is, how do you know what it is, or how do you know that it even exists?
> Obviously some things are better than others . . . but what's the betterness?"[20]

The *requirements and specifications* are detailed expressions of the project objectives. They will be the base for performing the project, and are the means to determine if the project was successful. For the most part, this requires the expectations to be not just known but written. To know something, without having it in writing, is too dangerous, particularly when we are basing the success of the project on the knowing. Our memories are very much improved when we write things down. The *product scope* is the sum of all the features and functions of the product. It is through the clear and "formal" description of the product in the form of requirements or specifications that we manage expectations.

Quality control is the process for making sure that project results are correct reflections of requirements. It consists of testing and reviewing. This is where the objective criteria that define quality are tested against the results to assess if the project delivered what was expected.

Quality assurance is the process to make sure that the process used to deliver the results is as effective as it can be. Quality control is past and present focused: Does the delivered product meet expectations? Quality assurance is future focused: Will we deliver products to meet expectations in the most effective way?

We will explore quality assurance and the quality of process later.

Here our focus is on the definition and assessment of the quality of the product.

The Two Kinds of Expectations

Expectations may be realistic or unrealistic.
Clinging to unrealistic expectations is the cause of suffering.

In projects there are a number of types of unrealistic expectations. One is where results are expected within unrealistic time and cost constraints because the constraints are not in keeping with the nature of the results, resources, and other factors. This is the class addressed in the chapters on estimating and risk.

In the other class of unrealistic expectations is the expectation that others will know what you expect without being explicitly told.

Then there is the belief that you know what others expect *without* being told.

Then there is the expectation that people will actually do what you expect of them.

The key to managing expectations is to first acknowledge that people always expect something and then to consciously and explicitly find out what it is.

How likely is it that a group of people performing a project will deliver what the sponsor and client want without being told what the sponsor and client want? How likely is it that a client, without being informed of the need to do so, will expect to spend a lot of time with project performers, informing them of his expectations and validating that they understand them as he does?

The answers are pretty obvious—the likelihood is small, and if it does occur, it is either by the skill, knowledge, and patience of the performers, or by luck.

Clever clients, sponsors, or managers will expect and insist upon a reasonable degree of time and effort to be spent managing expectations. But sometimes the client thinks (expects) that the project performers know what she wants. Sometimes the performers do know. Sometimes the performers think they know but really don't. Sometimes they don't know and know they don't know. In any case, managing expectations means to get the client to say what she expects, write it down, and then validate to make sure that there is mutual understanding. Then, as the project continues, make sure that change is managed to keep the expectations fresh and in keeping with current conditions.

In some cases finding out what the expectations are means simply asking, listening, expressing, and validating them. In other cases it means *intuiting* the expectations, expressing them to the client and others and then asking, listening, refining, and validating.

In either case, the expectations are formally expressed in concrete terms, in narratives, drawings, prototypes, and/or models. While it is better to express expectations orally than not at all, expressing them more formally is the practice *strongly* recommended. Formality avoids unnecessary changes and conflicts caused by misinterpretation and memory lapses.

Defining Objectives

By now it should be clear that in projects, the foundation for delivering quality results is defining realistic objectives and requirements. For example, the objective of a project may be to implement, within six months, a computer-supported system to streamline the way orders are processed in a company so that 99 percent of the orders are delivered within one day for a processing cost of less than $10. The objective for the implementation is to reduce operating costs by 50 percent within two years and to measurably improve customer satisfaction by 80 percent.

Note the difference between the project objectives (deliver or implement something within time and cost constraints) and the higher order objectives that represent the reasons that drive the project objectives. These higher order objectives are the results we described earlier, the expected benefits. In most cases, they are expected to be realized after the project is completed. They may be increased profits, better customer service, regulatory compliance, or service to the community.

Whether a Zen view or a systems perspective, the fact remains that in healthy organizations we don't do anything that is not directed at achieving the organization's highest goals—to service its market, either make or save money, and satisfy its internal need for resources (human and other).

The old paradigm of SMART objectives still works. Define objectives so that they are *S*imple (i.e., easily understood and broken out into a set of discrete items), *M*easurable, *A*chievable, *R*elevant (i.e., aligned with needs and strategies), and *T*ime bound. The *smarter* the objectives are, the more likely it is that there will be *clarity and ease* during the project and, particularly, afterward, when it is time to see if the project achieved what it set out to achieve.

Clarity and Ease

Clarity and ease are two characteristics of an effective work environment. They are intrinsic to the Zen way.

Clarity implies an objective, analytical, and systems-oriented view, unencumbered by preconditioned thinking. In the highest sense it means knowing experientially beyond the intellect.

Ease is the ability to maximize results with minimum wasted energy. It covers intrapersonal and interpersonal relationships and emotions as well as the more concrete concepts, tools, and methods. In the last chapter the sense of being in flow is explored. Ease means being in flow—dynamically engaged, able to sustain peak performance.

Defining Requirements and Specifications— Features, Functions and Behaviors

> Are you awake?
> Feel your body; your breath.
> How easy it is to get lost in the details. The wisdom practitioner "pops" out every so often to see the big picture. With practice, the 'popping out' occurs naturally.

As we drill down into the definition of requirements we are practicing the outer work. Remember, the outer work is about perfecting the form; doing things in the most efficient and effective way to get the desired outcome. As we do the outer work and confront our need for greater perfection, we have the opportunity to do the inner work of increasing our insight into the way our mind works and through that, coming closer to self-actualization.

Requirements describe the expected features, functions, and behaviors of the project outcome. Specifications are generally more detailed statements of requirements. For example, a requirement might say that a door with etched glass panes is required, and a specification would provide the exact measurements and perhaps other qualifications. Specifications generally result from design activities and are more detailed and precise than statements of requirements.

Getting All Parties to Comprehend and Agree

However, the distinctions among objectives, requirements, and specifications are by no means etched in glass or stone. In some projects, requirements and specifications are combined, while in other projects they are distinctly separate. Sometimes objectives are more detailed and overlap with requirements. Sometimes the product itself or a prototype takes the place of detailed requirements and specifications.

The key point is that as the complexity and criticality of the product increases, it is increasingly necessary to describe its requirements formally and in levels of detail. The goal is to make sure that all parties can fully comprehend and agree that there is an accurate and correct reflection of client expectations. Change in requirements is exponentially more expensive the farther along the project is. Requirements can evolve over a product's life. If this is by design, then it is probably skillful. If it is by accident, then it is not skillful and is sure to cause conflict.

Levels of Detail and "Progressive Elaboration"

The process of expressing expectations in levels of detail is *progressive elaboration.* It represents one of the most useful and elegant concepts in project management, knowledge management, and requirements definition.

The basic idea is to start at a fairly high level of detail and get agreement regarding the understanding of what is expected at that level. Then, based on the agreed upon high-level description, you describe the product in greater detail, agree upon that description and possibly refine the higher level description, taking it to a next level of detail. This may continue in levels of detail depending on the size and complexity of the product. This concept is like the breakdown of the work required in a project.

Given the limitations of the human mind and the inability of many people to concentrate for long on detailed information, it is best to present information in levels of detail. The highest level describes the big picture, and lower levels progressively describe complete "big pictures" of each of the parts of the total big picture. Recognize that the details must fully describe and not contradict the big picture and that the big picture is subject to change as the details are being defined. Figure 1 is a graphic example of how a complex end result might be divided up into bite-sized chunks to enable better understanding of the whole.

Figure 1 represents a hierarchical view of the product. Some products can be described in a more relational view, for example, describing

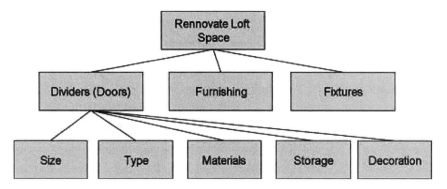

Figure 1. Levels of Detail

the requirements for a website in terms of the way its users will use it. Others are described in a less structured way but still with a clear understanding of progressive elaboration. Progressive elaboration enables clear thinking. It is the antidote for getting caught in the details and forgetting the big picture.

An Example

Here is an example of how progressive elaboration works: A client wants to divide a large loft into three distinct rooms while allowing light and air to flow throughout the space and permitting the dividers to be hidden from time to time to make the space look like it is undivided. That is the objective.

The contractor writes it down, and goes over it with the client, who says, "Yes, that's what I want." That takes no more than a few minutes for each of them. It can be done in person or via e-mail. It can also be done over the phone. In any case it should be in writing. Otherwise there is the risk of misunderstanding.

Next the contractor asks the client, "What did you have in mind for the dividers?" The client says, "glass sliding doors" and produces a lovely drawing of two large panels that extend from floor to ceiling and wall to wall. That is the next level of detail.

The contractor takes a look at the drawing and says how beautiful it is, but quickly gets down to making sure this level of detail is in keeping with the big picture (the objectives). He asks questions and informs the client of the realities associated with the space required for "hiding" the doors from time to time. They explore sliding door and swinging door options. The client likes the sliding option but must now settle for the loss of space on either side for storing the doors when they are open. Since glass isn't particularly bendable or roll-able, the storage space issue leads to exploring the possibility of dividing each side of the door to enable folding, using some other materials besides glass. Finally they settle on folding doors in four panels and "attractive" storage closets on each wall to store the open doors.

Then they turn to the client's desire for floor-to-ceiling doors and the issue of air flow. Clearly there is need for some transom or other means for ventilation. They think and discuss and come up with an acceptable idea that combines elegance, beauty, and practicality. It is possible that the client could have changed the original objectives and settled for a design that did not permit airflow between the spaces, but instead ventilated each space using a duct system hidden above the ceiling. If this had happened, it would have been necessary to revise the original understanding.

Risk Management in Action: Integrated Process

Before they are finished with this second level of detail, they must address framing the glass, weight, and breakability issues, and the ability to get the panels into the space (considering factors like elevator height limitations, and the size of doorways). Because the contractor has done this kind of project before, he knows what questions to ask.

Notice the transition from the big picture view to the details, and the progression to the next level only after the higher level has been explored and agreed upon.

This is risk management in action. Notice how the risk management is intertwined with the definition of the product and how the two relate to cost and time issues. Questioning the risks associated with each design option or feature helps the client to decide more effectively.

It helps to avoid disappointments later.

Remember, as much as it would be nice to be able to have a neat linear process, the reality is that estimating, scheduling, defining requirements, and risk management are all intertwined in an integrated process.

Imagine what could happen if risk assessment and analysis are not done as part of the requirements definition: The doors are done (at great expense) and delivered to the building; they don't fit through the front door; people start freaking out; they come up with a solution (hoist them up and in through a window (at more great expense); days go by before the hoisting can be done; during the hoisting they accidentally break the windows ….

Patience

All this is of course normal project management practice—well maybe not normal, but certainly good practice.

So where is the Zen? It comes into play as the definition process unfolds. Remember Pat? We described how she subtly changed the way she operated by asking questions and observing her internal and external experience so that she could be responsive and skillfully manage her situation. Here the practitioner repeats the same process but using more refined definitional and communication skills. Completeness and accuracy are heightened as project complexity increases. Precision and accuracy require time and effort, and these require patience.

Patience is the ability to abide with the discomfort of a moment without having to change it. Its etymology links it to suffering. According to Merriam-Webster, it is the ability to bear "pains or trials calmly without complaint." The "discomfort of the moment"—in the context of describing project requirements and the elements of quality results—is that complex of thoughts and feelings that arise when things are going too slow or in a way that is not the way you have in mind.

As these feelings arise, the same process we applied to fear and anger in earlier chapters is applied. When we want the project to get done quickly and as inexpensively as possible and are faced with the tedious process of describing details and getting agreements among people who have different views, communication styles, terminology, levels of intelligence, and skill, some will become impatient. The pressure of impatience becomes so intense that it causes the individual to perhaps rush ahead, become rude, lose the concentration required to be complete and accurate, among other negative behaviors. Can you recognize the experience of impatience in yourself? Have you "felt" it in others?

How do we work with impatience? There are several compatible approaches in the Zen way. One is to cultivate sufficient mindfulness to see the arising of impatience before it intensifies to the degree that it "takes over" and drives behavior. As you see impatience rising, you can change your mind by perhaps convincing yourself that the tedious process is well worth the effort and that it is in the best interest of project success. Here you are perfecting your performance through analysis and discipline. You can make a game of it. You can play with the idea that letting go of the final result to focus on the present moment is a very skillful way to concentrate on the task at hand. You stay in the moment. When impatience arises you recognize its source—wanting things to be different than they are—faster, better, easier. When you see this source you smile to yourself and get back to work—happily and patiently.

"Why the smile?" you might ask. The smile is a natural result of your recognition of the basic principle—suffering is the result of clinging to wanting things to be different from the way they are. It is the joy at being able to let go and relax in the moment.

Next Steps

Let's go back to our Glass Doors scenario. The contractor goes off and creates some drawings with related text to describe the resulting requirements. He reviews them with the client and they agree. The results of the second level of detail have changed the client's expectations. It has taken several hours across several days. The client is a little antsy, but the side story about the consequences of not taking the time to be precise makes it clear to him that patience and due diligence are worth it.

Next (sorry, we are still not finished) the contractor's people take precise measurements and create a detailed specification of the exact dimensions of the doors, complete with the location of hinges between panels, hand-holds for closing and opening, the storage closets, and the implications of the dimensions on the utilization of the space on either side of the doors. They discover that the requirements, as they have been stated, are not realistic because the size of the glass panels makes them very difficult and costly, if not impossible, to transport. More estimating and risk management. After some negotiating and redesigning, they resolve that issue and revise the requirements.

Fortunately, the client was very wealthy and patient, so price and time to complete were not issues. (This is a made up example; don't expect it to happen on any of your projects any time soon). Had time and price been issues, there might have been another round or two of changes to align the requirements with cost and time constraints.

To make matters even more complex, the manufacturer's requirements, and even the requirements of the people who will be maintaining the doors, would need to be considered.

What Could Have Happened?

In this example, the contractor and client cooperated effectively. They took the time to explore and negotiate. The client changed his expectations and spent the time needed to get the definition. The contractor was patient. The client was patient.

Imagine what might have happened if the contractor took the original objectives and unilaterally created a workable solution. The client might have accepted the design and just loved it, congratulating the contractor and giving him a bonus for being so clever and effective.

On the other hand, the client might have reacted badly, rejecting the results because they did not satisfy his original expectations regarding cost, time and design. How might your client respond or react if you took it upon yourself to deliver a workable solution that does not fully satisfy expectations? How would you, if you were the client?

"Why would the contractor unilaterally create a solution?" you might ask. Among the possible reasons might be that the client was unavailable to take part in a dialogue and the contractor wanted to get the job done. Another possibility is that the contractor thought that the client would understand the need for a practical solution and accept the contractor's clever way to deliver.

Quality Characteristics and Acceptance

If quality is the degree to which a result satisfies expectations and is fit for use, then we can see that our example addresses only half the story. The definition of requirements sets and documents the expectations. The delivery of the results and evaluation by the client, using the documented requirements as criteria, determine if quality has been achieved.

In order to formally enable the evaluation of the product, requirements and specifications must include every aspect of the product that will be used in the evaluation. The requirements must address all of the quality characteristics. Quality characteristics are the behaviors, features, and functions of the product. They are the criteria upon which the product's degree of quality is based.

In our example, quality characteristics would include ease of opening and closing the doors, the degree of difficulty in getting the doors into the building, the exactness of replication of the etched design, the beauty of the storage closets, the way they match other design elements, the color of the glass, and more.

If we have a process like the one in the example, it is likely that these elements will be addressed. But to make sure, it is best to go into the requirements definition with a checklist of relevant elements rather than relying on the expertise and memory of the project performers, contractors, or others.

Note that a complete, formal and detailed specification document is *not* absolutely necessary. The project team, the manager, client, and sponsor explicitly or implicitly agree to a degree of formality and detail. Of course the more informal and the less detailed, the greater the risk. More on this topic in the chapter on process.

Subjectivity—Managing Individual Taste

I'll know what I want when I see it.

The area of quality is never particularly straightforward. Subjectivity is unavoidable when issues like beauty, ease of use, the way different design elements match one another, look, and feel are involved as criteria for accepting the product.

Subjectivity is the opposite of objectivity. A subjective view is based on individual taste and attitude. Subjective views are subject to change depending on the conditions affecting the individual. For example, the individual's mood or exposure to a new model that triggers ideas about the aesthetic goodness of a design or product feature can affect the degree to which a previously acceptable outcome may no longer be acceptable. We are fickle.

The changeability of subjective views is an issue in project work. It leads to changes in the middle of projects (for example, "Change the color," "make this bigger") and worse, causes disputes at the project's completion because expectations have changed and acceptance of the project result is not easily obtained. In the end, satisfying the client (a principle success criterion) depends on the client's subjective view of the outcome.

Managing subjectivity requires first acknowledging it. Once acknowledged, the subjective criteria should be stated as requirements. Time must be spent exploring the means for testing to see if the criteria are met by the results. The client must acknowledge that change to these requirements, as with all requirements, may create delays and costs for the project. The project team might design the product so as to easily adapt to changing tastes, if possible.

> Do not think that just because a quantified set of specific acceptance criteria—like size, weight, speed,—have been met that the client will be satisfied.

For example, in a project to implement a customer service call center, success criteria included metrics like response time, number of return calls on the same issue, number of minutes on hold waiting for service, as well as customer satisfaction. The project result was measured over the first six months of operation and all quantitative metrics were found to be well within acceptable parameters. Yet, customer satisfaction was lower than desired. Upon exploring the cause of the customer satisfaction shortfall, it was discovered that customers disliked the tone of voice and demeanor of the greeting and directions announcement that preceded contact with a live representative. Some complained about the insipid music played during wait periods (others thought the music was fine).

In retrospect, the project team that created the call center realized that they did not consider the aesthetics of the voice and music components. Had they considered these, they would have established a requirement and acceptance criterion that these features be attractive to a large proportion of callers. They would have tested to make sure that those criteria had been achieved.

In the Zen way we emphasize clarity, objectivity, and the ability to stand back from one's own subjectivity. At the same time we accept the reality of subjectivity. It is operating in and around us as long as we are individuals with egos. By acknowledging it as a normal part of the process, we can more effectively manage the situation.

Without having a totally objective set of acceptance criteria, how can we manage the project? We use our intuition. We get to know the client and the sponsor. We get a sense of who they are and what they like. We relax our analytical left brain and allow our right brain to come to the surface. We communicate regularly and in a meaningful way to make sure that progress is being made and that it is appreciated.

Combining Words, Drawings, Prototypes, and Models

"There's no question that photographs communicate more instantly and powerfully than words do, but if you want to communicate a complex concept clearly, you need words, too."

Galen Rowell[21]

"Designers can create normalcy out of chaos; they can clearly communicate ideas through the organizing and manipulating of words and pictures."

Jeffrey Veen[22]

"I'll know what I want when I see it."

This simple phrase has long been a cause of frustration for project managers. Well, it need not be. When it comes to setting requirements, particularly when the product is a complex one and there are aesthetic and behavioral issues, it is often impossible to describe the product in writing. The language of words is limited. That is why the client in our doors example started with a picture and the contractor communicated through drawings. Graphical representations—drawings, blueprints, and three dimensional computer-generated graphics—are wonderful means for describing complex, hard to describe things, but they are also limited by the needs and thinking styles of different viewers (some people do better with words than pictures; sometimes pictures leave much to the imagination).

Prototypes and models are other means for communicating complex concepts. Prototypes are generally models that represent an envisioned product. They exhibit product behaviors, look and feel, and other characteristics in a way that can never be done in words. They take pictures and not only put them in motion, they enable the client to interact with the prototype to get a sense of how the product will behave when it is finished. In our example, the contractor could have built a scale model of the space, with the doors in place and moveable to show how they open and close and what they will look like. In developing computer systems like websites and applications of many kinds, it is quite common for the developers to create prototypes based on relatively informal discussions with clients and then refine them through further discussion. The cost of doing this is low compared with the cost of writing down the specifications, verifying them with the client, developing the product, and then dealing with the inevitable responses, like "I didn't know it would look like that. Change it."

Use the right combination of narrative, graphics, models, and prototypes to communicate.

Limitations of Linear Thinking

Recognize the limitations of linear, analytical thinking. Language is linear and analytical and, of course, very powerful as a means to communicate. But words are only one means, and in terms of communication, they convey a very small proportion of the full meaning. Use nonanalytical methods—pictures, working models, prototypes.

If you question the premise that language is very limited as a means to determine requirements, try to describe in words the way a voice or piece of music will sound over a telephone or via computer. If you had an important client who was choosing the sounds that would greet his or her customers or employees, would you rely on words or would you sample the sounds and play them, perhaps modifying them or offering several selections to choose one that is pleasing?

Use your eyes and intuition along with your ears and intellect when working to come to agreement with others. Body language, the look on someone's face, their tone of voice, and other, less definable inputs often tell the discerning "listener" what others are really thinking.

Be ready to reconcile contradictory inputs. You might say something like "I have a sense that you are not really happy with that idea; maybe we should look at some other options before deciding." The project manager is often driven by desire to "get it done," so suggesting that a client think about other options when he is ready to buy (based on his own words) is counterintuitive. Do it anyway. In the end, it will save time and trouble. Remember, changes late in the project cost lots more than changes during the time when requirements are being discussed and defined and designs are being developed.

Be in the moment. That is a fundamental Zen principle. If the moment is right for defining requirements, then that's what you do. If it is about opening up to diverse possibilities, then do that. When it is the time to pick one way to go, then do that. How do you know when it is right to do what? At first you use a guide or procedure. As you master your art, you just know.

The master does not overdo it. Always, there is the need for dynamic balance.

Priorities and Tradeoffs

Getting everything you want is rare. In projects the norm is to make tradeoffs in order to create a realistic balance among results, cost, and time constraints. Given the availability of resources and money and the inability to magically manifest desired outcomes, it is usually necessary to cut back on some features or functions and/or to settle for less than what is really wanted.

If tradeoffs are agreed upon in a rational and mutually acceptable way, expectations are managed and the key stakeholders will not be disappointed when the product is delivered. Remember, unrealistic expectations cause suffering. If expectations are managed they will be realistic.

To best prepare for the negotiations that lead to tradeoff agreements, prioritize requirements. What are the must-haves? Among the nice-to-haves (everything other than the must-haves), which are most nice to have, least nice to have, and which are in-between? There are many possible prioritization scales with three, five, or a hundred gradations in nice-to-have-ness. Pick one that makes sense for your project. And use it to get the client and relevant others (e.g., sponsor, product owners and custodians) to rank requirements' priorities. For example, is having airflow through the doors a must have, or, alternatively, where does it fall on a scale of one (not really that important) to five (very, very important). Knowing will make it easier to make the decision as to whether to have a transom within the doors vs. duct work to ventilate the closed off areas, when the time comes.

Note that because many requirements are subjective (e.g., the aesthetically based desire to have a complete pane rather than one encumbered by a transom or some other mechanism to allow airflow), it is likely that the priorities will change when the decision needs to be made. In our example, at the very start the complete pane requirement may have been quite high in priority. When faced with the cost and complexity of alternatives, the priority may change, particularly if there is a reasonably attractive alternative.

Making trade-offs requires letting go of preconceived ideas and opening the mind to new possibilities. It also requires a realistic attitude regarding cost, time, benefits, and risk issues. The Zen approach seeks to clear away unfounded beliefs and conditioning to see things as they are. This allows for seeing things as they can be.

Binding Decisions & Consensus

Negotiation, tradeoffs, multiple stakeholders to satisfy—these all add up to the need to make decisions. Relatively binding decisions regarding requirements need to be made fairly early in projects. Otherwise there will be conflict and costly changes later.

Note the difference between a "meeting of the minds" and a binding decision. In a binding decision there is a sincere intention to hold to the decision into the future, in the face of changing conditions. Legal contracts are binding in that they hold the parties liable for damages caused by noncompliance. Any agreement about project objectives, requirements, and specifications is part of the project contract (whether legally binding or not).

Here, in the difference between binding and nonbinding, is another example of dynamic balance. If the binding is too rigid, then there will be difficulty when conditions change. If there is no binding then there is likely to be random change by any of the parties, causing avoidable conflict and excessive costs and delays.

Consensus decisions are those in which all parties *truly* agree to the conclusion and are satisfied that it meets their needs (if not their initial wants). Consensus is usually best among decision-making alternatives, though the cost and time it takes to reach consensus is often excessive.

The alternatives range from authority-based directives (which may or may not be wisely made) by individuals or small groups to democratic decisions in which a majority decides (invariably dissatisfying the minority, to at least some degree).

To effectively manage expectations, it is best to agree about the way decisions will be made and to agree to the degree to which the decisions are to be binding on all parties. Experience tells us that just because people agree to something it does not mean they will continue to agree. That's why there are contracts and courts.

From the Zen perspective successful negotiation and decision-making is conditioned by the degree to which the participants can let go of their preconceived ideas. This ability to let go and allow the flow of events (influenced by dialogue, preferences, analysis and other elements) to take their course is a critical success factor.

Controlled Changed

Change is inevitable. Effective agreements recognize and prepare for change.

Since everything is subject to change, we need to control change to the degree that we can. We want to enable positive change while keeping unnecessary and undesirable change to a minimum.

> PARADOX:
> Change is inevitable. We need to just let the flow carry us.
> But, changes will delay the project, increase costs, and increase risk. We need to eliminate them.
> The middle way is to enable positive change and eliminate undesirable change.

Changes, up to a point, are part of the negotiation of project requirements, costs, and schedules. Once there is agreement, a *baseline* is set. The baseline is the agreed upon scope, time, and cost for the project. It is called a baseline because it is used as a point of comparison to assess progress and completion.

But changes will not stop after the agreement to the scope. As the desire or need for change arises, it is addressed in a consciously designed process. The change control process evaluates each change based on cost, risk, and reward. Decision makers with the right level of authority for the scope and impact of a change decide whether and when the change should be made. Schedules and budgets are adjusted to compensate for the time and effort required to make the change. Note this last statement—it is about keeping the estimates and schedules realistic. Changes take work. Work costs time and money. There is always interplay among time, cost, and scope. Risk is always part of the equation.

Note that change control is work and that it is not necessarily viewed as beneficial by clients and project performers. They want the autonomy and fluidity to make the product right through a natural dialogue across the life of the project. The client and performers will naturally see things that they want or have to change (note the difference). They don't want to be encumbered by a bureaucratic process to describe, assess, decide and then have their change rejected or postponed. They just want to do it.

Just doing it is not a problem if time and money are not issues. My friend renovated his house. During the construction he made adjustments in the design—things like where windows were to be placed. If you know anything about construction, this is expensive and time consuming. But my friend was getting a real sense of the way the house would look and he could afford the time and money. The contractor grumbled about it but in the end was fine with it.

In most of the real world, time and money are pretty important. Enable positive change and eliminate undesirable change. We need to control change to make sure that the product is useful and satisfying when delivered but also that it is delivered within time and cost constraints. Expectations must be met for the project to be successful.

> Patience in the early stages of the project pays off later. The more effectively objectives and requirements are defined and designs are created, the less the likelihood of change.

Quality Control—Making Sure the Outcome Meets Expectations

> The earlier a defect is detected, the easier it is to correct.

Quality control (QC) is the process of evaluating the product against expectations to determine if it complies. Testing, inspections, reviews, and actual use are the means for QC. QC feeds information back into the planning and requirements definition process so that expectations can be kept realistic. QC is costly and time consuming, particularly when you account for the fixes that are needed when defects are found.

Some people may argue with the statement that *"QC is always present in every project."* They may remember projects in which the product was created and rolled out into regular use without testing. But even in these projects, someone is evaluating the results against expectations.

When this is done during the operational use of the product, it is a sign of poor judgment *or* a calculated risk. The calculated risk is based on thinking, "We can save the time, effort, and expense of testing and trade that off against the possibility of dissatisfied clients and sponsors. We can fix any defects when we find them in operational use."

In the end, the client and sponsor will evaluate the results against their expectations. QC is one part of managing expectations. It helps to keep the project on track to deliver an outcome that meets clients' and sponsors' needs and expectations. Effective QC identifies defects and shortfalls so that they can be addressed with minimum impact on cost and schedule.

It is good to remember that defects and shortfalls in project results remain in the memories of clients and sponsors. It affects their confidence in the project manager and the degree to which they want to pay the bills for the current project as well as future ones. Further, the cost of correcting defects after the project is far higher than the cost of fixing them during the project, and the cost of avoiding them is often much less than the cost of fixing them.

Defects and shortfalls usually need <u>not</u> be corrected to satisfy expectations. Expectations are changeable. If a client expects defects that have been consciously left in a product for good reason, they are likely to be accepting of them, even if they are disruptive. If there are shortfalls like undelivered features or late delivery, which are communicated upfront, expectations can be renegotiated. The perfect flawless product is a goal, but not necessarily one that needs to be reached in a project. Don't spoil the good by perfectionism. The Zen potter plants a flaw as a reminder that perfection includes imperfection.

QC is standard PM wisdom. There is nothing special about it. Yet there are issues. It takes time and effort. It is hard to estimate. It means criticizing someone's work product.

The Zen PM applies patience to make sure there is due diligence even when the target date is coming up quickly and the rushing mind is saying things like "everything seems so perfect, we don't really need to review it or test it."

People identify with their products. When the products are criticized and found to be full of holes some will take it personally. Here is an opportunity for compassion and for letting go of the identification with one's products. Can you be open to criticism and learn from it? Can you be ruthless in your critique and compassionate at the same time? In the Zen way, the performer can separate from the performance. She is not threatened by criticism. She invites it and uses it as a means for growth. Even the arising of fear and anger – common reactions to criticism – become signals for self exploration and self-actualization.

Delivering and Accepting the Results

Products are delivered through projects. Results are achieved by using products.

When objectives, requirements, and specifications are mutually understood, clear, and well defined, and there are agreed upon quality control and change control processes, the product delivery will be relatively smooth.

When the product is delivered, it is best to get concrete, formal, and definitive acknowledgement of acceptance from clients and sponsors. Don't assume that just because the project manager thinks he's done, the client agrees. If there is any dissatisfaction, it needs to be addressed. Even when there are legally binding contracts with very explicit specifications and objective measures, there are disputes about acceptance.

> Quality is ultimately subjective. People change their minds.

Acceptance and closure are not just for the end of the project. Important steps are performed in the life of every project—there is a design, there are parts of the product that can be evaluated, there may be prototypes. The outcomes of each of these steps [23]should be evaluated and accepted. This enables communication and reaffirmation of expectations or identification of the need for change—managing expectations. Incremental acceptance throughout the project will pretty much guarantee easy acceptance at the end.

Recap

> **Unrealistic expectations are a root cause of project failure.**

No one (except project managers) wants projects. *Results* are what people want. Often, the *real* results are delivered well after a project is complete. The project delivers a product that is then used or sold to achieve some higher order objective— for example, making more money, or enjoying productive and pleasant occupancy of a new facility, home, or office.

Both subjective and objective criteria must be considered in any exchange. If client satisfaction is a principle success factor, then the subjective satisfaction of the client must be considered and managed. Unrealized expectations are at the root of dissatisfaction.

> **We suffer when we don't get what we expect to get. In project work, we suffer when other people don't get what *they* expect.**

Managing expectations is the foundation for delivering quality results. Quality means satisfying requirements and expectations to deliver an outcome that is fit for use. To deliver quality, the best practice approach makes sure there are sufficient resources, effective method, time, and effort to get a mutual understanding of the expected results —delving into the subtle details that may seem unimportant at the beginning of the project but can become difficult issues at the end. The mutual understanding of expectations includes the hard-to-define subjective elements, roles to be played, and concrete objectives associated with well-defined requirements.

In the end, communication toward a mutual understanding of the expectations of all parties to the project, coupled with a process to insure that those expectations are realistic, provides the key to project success. The project manager as well as clients and sponsors are most likely to succeed if they set realistic expectations. This means combining written statements of requirements and acceptance criteria, drawings, prototypes, and models to get a meeting of the minds about what results are expected. It means that roles and responsibilities are well defined and that there is realistic expectation regarding change. It also means that the elements of risk management, quality management, estimating, and scheduling are integrated fully with the management of the project's scope.

Defining objectives and requirements is a Zen art within the Zen art of PM. Impatience, attachment, and frustration stand in the way of defining requirements. These provide the opportunities for the inner work, and the inner work makes the outer work easier, more enjoyable, and more effective.

The product is the result of a process. The process is performed by individuals usually working in teams. Perfect the process and the product will be perfect. Not too perfect, of course, but, perfectly addressing the needs of the situation, the inevitability of a degree of imperfection, and the relative cost of each degree of perfection. The next chapters address the quality of individual performance and process quality.

Chapter 7

Quality Performance and People

> Use your day-to-day activities as a means to the end of increased mindfulness, concentration, and calm. Are you consciously aware of your reading?

Purpose

This chapter is put between the chapters on product quality and process quality to highlight the critical importance of individual attitude. People, of course, are ourselves, our teams and our organizations. We, as those people, are on a journey. As we travel, it is our responsibility to keep from getting lost.

> Are you awake? Are you clear about your destination, your goals? Whose goals are they? Who is asking?

Quality

Quality has a number of facets. *Quality control* (QC), as we have seen, directs the vision to the outcome to answer the questions: "Does the product meet its quality criteria? Does it comply with its specifications? Do its specifications satisfy the needs and expectations of product stakeholders? To what degree?"

Quality assurance (QA) directs the vision to the process to answer the questions: "Are we working in the best possible way? Do we have a well-defined, practical, continuously improving process being performed by people with the right capabilities in a supportive environment?" This will be addressed more fully in the next chapter.

This chapter examines the difference between mediocre and excellent performance. If we look at the need for sustained performance excellence across multiple projects, we see that it is based on building an ongoing team of people with increasingly high capability to perform. The focus of this chapter is on defining, valuing, and leveraging excellent performers.

Performance Excellence

Performance excellence is the ability to consistently deliver high quality results within time/cost constraints to satisfy the needs and expectations of stakeholders. It is measured by whether or not criteria, including subjective ones like client and performer satisfaction, are satisfied.

Performance excellence is one end of a continuum. The other is unacceptable performance—performance that consistently results in outcomes that significantly miss meeting expectations. Unacceptable performance, like excellent performance, is a measurable yet subjective characteristic.

Performance excellence is relative and subjective because its definition changes based on external conditions that include individual perceptions, group perceptions, and any standards (stated or not) that are applied. For example, a few non-critical bugs in a product may be perfectly acceptable, but the definition of what is and is not critical and what "a few" means is subject to opinions and conditions, such as how the product will be used.

In the case of an advertisement for an event, a misspelling in the event title and the wrong time date and place are, in my opinion, unacceptable. One instance of such a defect out of tens of thousands of events may be acceptable.

In the case of an "O" ring in a spacecraft, the instance of a single defect that causes the craft to crash and burn is hard to accept. I won't say "unacceptable" because we know it has occurred and we accept it can possibly occur again. That is why we spend so much time reaching for high quality performance.

A typo or two in an e-mail to a colleague is considered acceptable by most people. If the colleague is also a client, the tolerance level for the acceptable level of typos may be less than the level for teammates.

In some firms, the perception of excellence is left up to the performers, while in others there is a continuous attempt to determine the perceptions of the client and others to arrive at a broader based understanding of what excellence is. One can think one's performance is excellent, but unless that is tested through expanded benchmarking and one gets candid feedback from others, one does not really know.

Mediocrity

Somewhere between the extremes of excellent and unacceptable is mediocre. Mediocre is a loaded word; that is, it brings up an emotional response in many people (me for instance). It has a pejorative sense to it. Some people will be more comfortable with terms like *ordinary* or *acceptable.* Whatever we call it, the more acceptable we make *mediocre,* the less likelihood we have of reaching excellence. We want excellence to be ordinary.

It is important to realize that excellent does <u>not</u> mean expensive. Many will agree that Rolls Royce and Porsche build excellent cars. But we must also recognize that many far less costly cars are also excellent, given their cost-performance ratio. When it comes to performance excellence, the cost of performance plus the overall cost of using, supporting, and enhancing the product is less than the equivalent cost of mediocre performance.

The People Factor

Quality begins with people who share a common vision. People are the key factor in performance excellence. They not only define the criteria for determining what excellence is; they establish and manage the performance process and its supporting systems, they perform the process, and they evaluate the results.

In addition to having many different opinions about what excellence is, people have vastly different capacities to perform, ranging from superstardom to inadequate. Inadequate performers can be accepted as is, upgraded through training and coaching, or eliminated. The population in the middle—adequate performers—may be upgraded, depending on their capacity. Note that adequate performers may be excellent in some ways, and that superstars may be mediocre in some ways. Even superstars have something to learn.

But in the end, the degree of capacity should be consciously chosen to meet the need. Constitutional lawyer Jack Balkin states:

"When Richard Nixon nominated G. Harold Carswell in 1969 to be a Supreme Court Justice, many people pointed out Carswell's less than stunning qualifications. Senator Roman Hruska, a conservative politician from Nebraska, attempted to turn this into an asset: 'Even if he is mediocre,' Hruska contended, 'there are a lot of mediocre judges and lawyers. They are entitled to a little representation, aren't they, and a little chance? We can't have all Brandeises, Cardozos, and Frankfurters, and stuff like that there.'"

Lots of people made fun of Hruska for saying that, and he's gone down in history for being a champion of mediocrity. What we want on the federal bench above all is good judgment. Good judgment is not the same thing as great legal acuity or legal brilliance.[24]

Hopefully, we agree that the performance quality expected on your projects is sufficiently high for you, your clients and your sponsors. Who would opt for a mediocre surgeon for our own operation or the operation of a loved one?

This is of course a touchy area. It brings up all sorts of feelings in some, ranging from happiness, self appreciation, and fulfillment of one's need for recognition; to anger and indignation, fear and disappointment, among others. Excellent fuel for the inner work.

Criteria for People's Performance Quality

Now, if we accept that quality should be measurable based on criteria, there is a need for a set of criteria by which to measure. How do we differentiate the superstars from the acceptable performers and identify the inadequate performers. Further, we need a means for identifying excellence in people's behavior, as opposed to their ability to perform as superstars.

What is a superstar? According to Jay Lorsch and Thomas Tierney in *Aligning the Stars,*[25] stars are the "individuals with the highest future value to the organization." Stars may be anywhere in the organization, playing any role. Stardom is defined based on industry and client criteria and not just in comparison to one's peers in the organization. "Being a B student in a class of C students does not make one a star." In the end, clients decide which performers are great, which are just good, and which are unacceptable.

Experience has shown that the star is often "a natural" who, with the proper training and understanding, can perform faster and better than others. The star designer can "see" and articulate the elegant design effortlessly (or so it seems to the observer). The star customer service representative makes the clients feel fully cared for, as though they were the only ones being served.

There is a certain Zen quality to the star's performance. It seems effortless; the performance is performing itself.

Excellence vs. Stardom

But as we said, there is a difference between being a star and being an excellent performer. Some stars are prima donnas and others are the most delightful, cooperative people you ever would want to meet. Behavioral excellence is about the way the individual relates with others, their emotional intelligence—and the way they improve.

Consider the following situation that occurred in a recent project:
A functional manager (FM) responsible for producing published

material to support a product decides to change the sequence of writing, editing, format finalization, and final edit. He has the author send the material to him and does the formatting and proofing first in order to expedite the development. He does this without informing the product manager, who is responsible for content approval and the project budget.

When the product manager e-mails the author to find out when to expect the copy, he is informed by the functional manager of the change with a note that says, "If you're ready to do a final review, I can get the files to you."

The product manager responds with "I am not ready to do a final review as I have not done an initial review. When did we change the game on this one? First, I was supposed to review the modules one at a time, then all at once; now, is this an example of our commitment to quality control and collaboration and communication? Have we learned nothing from past experience?"

The FM's response is, "I really wish you would stop all of this complaining again. It doesn't serve anything except to continue causing aggravation and conflict."

Performance Excellence, Attitudes and Behavioral Skills

How does this vignette relate to individual performance excellence and Zen inner work?

Regardless of the degree to which any of the parties are stars, the attitude that "complaining" is a cause of "aggravation and conflict" rather than an opportunity to explore the behaviors or results that underlie the complaint, is a sure sign that the performer is <u>not</u> yet an excellent performer. Why? Because such an attitude is a direct barrier to performance improvement. The capacity for performance to improve is one of the critical criteria of performance excellence.

Yet, from a Zen perspective we have to look at all aspects of the issue if we seek objectivity. Was there a complaining tone? Was there a pressure to get done and shorten the process? What were the feeling tones and the facts of the matter? In the clarity of an objective, non-emotion driven mind, what is the right way to proceed?

Whether they are stars or not, excellent performers know the difference between the content of the work, the process for performing the work, and the interpersonal and intrapersonal processes that enable performance improvement and the cultivation of healthy relationships. As Belkin reminds us, good judgment is a critical differentiator. So is the ability to monitor and control one's emotions and to reflect the needs of others in one's behavior.

Attitudes regarding quality improvement and quality control are key to project performance. They impact the way individual projects—and all future projects—are performed.

Can we accept mediocrity in this people-dimension of quality? Sure, we can. We often find ourselves in situations that require us to accept the people we are assigned to work with -- people we may even select ourselves. As an example, I once hired an assistant who was just out of school but had worked as an assistant in her school. I thought she had the ability to quickly learn my requirements and do a good job. After a relatively short time I found that she was not up to the job and had lied about having kept up with some important work. I had to accept that and find a way to replace her as quickly as possible. I had to accept. I would have to live with the situation until the time was right to make a change.

Many, if not most, organizations fail to cultivate the awareness of interpersonal and intrapersonal processes and their critical importance to overall performance excellence—in and around projects. In fact, many organizations are so sluggishly or frantically doing what they do that they do not even cultivate awareness of the relationship between their process for performing the work and their content.

For organizations, whether they are departments, project teams, or entire enterprises, to excel, they must clearly identify the criteria for excellent performance and move away from merely accepting mediocrity. This requires training and cultural change. Training and cultural change in turn require recognition that change is needed and possible.

This author believes that the first step to performance excellence in any organization or team is awareness of the value of people who can perform at least adequately and who have the skills and capacity to self improve and relate well with others. These critical skills can be cultivated, though as always, there is a continuum. Here, it is of learning capacity. Identify the time and cost required to cultivate these skills in each individual. Some people will get it quickly, some more slowly, and others won't get it at all.

The excellent organization recognizes stardom and performance excellence and leverages them to ensure the organization's continuing ability to perform.

Here we have the Zen principle of acceptance balanced by applying skillful means in order to approach perfection. The Zen project manager accepts the way things are and manages by adapting to the needs and capabilities of the people on the team. At the same time, she creates attitudes and a system that promote continuous improvement.

Performance Appraisal

> "Performance stands out like a ton of diamonds. Nonperformance can always be explained away."
>
> Harold S. Geneen[26]

Performance appraisal recognizes and cultivates performance excellence. Performance appraisal is implied by the need to recognize and cultivate performance excellence. It is one of the most difficult and controversial aspects of organizational life.

Many management and leadership experts believe that the individual should evaluate his or her own progress and achievements based on candid feedback from peers (including both internal and external clients), superiors, and subordinates. The feedback should be primarily fact-based, but also include impressions and feelings.

Self assessment and assessment by peers and clients are the most valuable because they are based on direct experience. Assessment by subordinates, particularly direct reports, is next in usefulness, while assessment by superiors is usually least effective because it is generally considered to be based on secondhand information. The latter is mitigated, however, by the fact that in many cases the superior is operating as a peer or client and has direct working contact with the individual.

This 360 degree approach to performance appraisal, when supported by effective systems, training, and a trust-based environment, is reputed to be quite effective. However, it is not easy to put into practice in many environments.

Resistance to Candid Appraisal

In a small experiment, a man sent out an informal request to a number of peers for candid feedback regarding his performance, particularly the way he interacted with them. Of the twenty-five requests, he got three responses. One actually gave some useful and insightful feedback and the other two provided input about how best to do performance reviews. These last two responded but avoided the issue. The others simply ignored the initial request and a subsequent reminder. When he explored his peers' resistance, it boiled down to two underlying issues. One was lack of time and interest. The others were fear that they in turn would have to be evaluated by their peers if the process was institutionalized, and fear of retribution for negative feedback.

In the project management realm, the usual common organizational structure makes the appraisal of individual performers even more difficult than it is in non-project work. Most commonly, the performers on a project do not report directly to the project manager. They are often "on loan" from a functional manager or work for a subcontractor or are part of the client's organization. Unless there is a formal review process in which performance feedback is gathered from the PM, fellow team members, clients, and peers, it is unlikely that there will be any real appraisal. When the PM takes it upon him or herself to appraise contributors and the appraisal is negative, there are often significant "ripples."

To temporarily get around this problem, one can institute self-appraisal and peer appraisal as a voluntary, self improvement process within a project team. This is done by getting agreement from the team at the project's onset and setting up a simple process. The process should be based on a formal model, examples of which can be obtained from sources such as Decision Wise and Balance 360. In any event, there MUST be clearly defined criteria and a sense of safety, objectivity, and security.

But while voluntary appraisals may be helpful in improving personal performance, they do not really address the issue of improving organizational performance through the improvement of personal performance.

Stephen Covey says, "Sometimes facing reality is difficult, especially when hearing it from others. But we demean and insult other people when we treat them as anyone other than accountable, responsible, choice-making individuals. If, in the name of being nice and kind, we start protecting them, we begin the process of codependency and silent conspiracy that eventually results in the lowest level of initiative."[27]

In the end, to best serve the needs of individuals, projects, and organizations, a formal and intelligent appraisal process is needed to support performance excellence. From a pure project management perspective, this means enabling the appraisals of project managers and the appraisal of all other project contributors on a project by project basis, and consolidating the results to enable the evaluation of personal performance across multiple projects over time. From a Zen perspective, this is an essential element in the search for self-actualization. The seeker appreciates feedback, positive or negative, that enables improvement. Until one has the capacity to be entirely objective and all-seeing, it is only through the eyes of others that we can see ourselves.

Competency Development

"Learning is not compulsory. . . . neither is survival."
W. Edwards Deming[28]

In the project management world there is a growing interest in competency development, and the appraisal process that it implies. The Project Management Institute (PMI®) has published a Competency Development Framework that addresses the improvement of the performance of project personnel.

The framework is based on a model that sees the need for a combination of technical and personal competencies and their application. According to PMI's Project Manager Competency Development (PMCD) Framework, competence, when applied in the project management context, has three dimensions:

1. the knowledge and understanding of project management
2. the demonstrable ability to perform
3. behavior based on attitudes and core personality traits that individuals bring to the performance.

The model then drills down into a number of specific competencies and performance criteria. This model is directed at people who do project management. But ideally, there should be a model for the competencies of every project performer. This sets the stage for people to perform to the expected level of competence as well as for reasonably objective assessment.

Cultivating Knowledge

If projects are to be performed well, personal excellence must be cultivated. This implies the availability of knowledge to support performance. That knowledge comes in the form of training, coaching, and just-in-time support, such as knowledge bases that include templates, checklists, and procedures to help guide performers through their processes.

As a client or sponsor who is relying on the competence of a project manager and performance team, it is your responsibility to take the time and effort to ensure that you are on solid ground. Check references, review process descriptions, interview. Do not assume that just because someone calls him- or herself a project manager, they are one. Even people who are certified as project management professionals may not be competent. Buyer beware!

As an individual project manager, it is ultimately your responsibility to achieve personal competency. You may do so either by being part of an organization that is committed to performance excellence through the cultivation of personal excellence or by taking on the task unilaterally. Again we have a continuum and the need to face facts. Some people complain when their company fails to provide proper training and support. The Zen practitioner sees things as they are and takes personal responsibility to act in a way that satisfies the needs of the situation. If complaining louder works that's fine. If not, go out and get what you need.

Self-actualization and Zen

> "What a man can be, he must be. This need we call self-actualization."
> Abraham Maslow[29]

On the most personal level, self-actualization is the highest goal. In the Zen tradition, all goals and achievements are ultimately relinquished for an experience of intrinsic perfection. Self-actualization is the last achievement to be relinquished, since even attachment to the highest goal is still clinging; there is someone being attached to something. Being attached or clinging is having a feeling and strong motivation to keep, get or avoid something. For example, if I am attached to self-actualization I am motivated to achieve it. If I am attached to getting my way, I might be angry or unhappy at least some of the time. In the Zen way, the principle barrier to self-actualization is clinging or attachment.

Self-actualization is of course a very positive motivation. It is one of the last attachments one would want to let go of. But, in the highest sense, we achieve self-actualization by dropping away the barriers to seeing clearly. By doing so, we realize that there is nothing to achieve; it has been here all along. There is no solid "I" to achieve it.

In the Zen way, when we stop clinging we experience intrinsic perfection and are free, in the sense that a Buddha is free. *Note that it may take quite a long time (perhaps many lifetimes) to reach this level.* The journey is what we have now. It is like a continuous improvement process in which we keep approaching perfection until we realize that we have achieved it simply by having a continuous improvement process.

Explore the relationship you have with yourself. Go back to the basic questions—Who am I? Who is asking?

When we seek the mind with mind, we see that there is a continuously changing collection of causes and conditions. We see a process as opposed to something solid.

The need for self-actualization is in everyone, though it is often subordinated to the needs for recognition, social interaction, security, and survival. In the search for perfection that underlies the wisdom traditions, self-actualization is continuously remembered as the principle motivation. It is not competing against the other needs, and there is no need to subordinate it to them. We do that only when we are unmindful and out of touch with our wisdom.

When we explore self-actualization, what emerges are levels of "competency" that can be cultivated to let us "be what we can be." These levels are:

1. Compassionate action for the benefit of all;
2. Personal behavior through effective communications and relationships; and

3. Performance excellence through continuous improvement of one's process.

The path to self-actualization is founded on taking personal responsibility to combine the elements of ethical behavior, wisdom, and the cultivation of mindfulness and concentration.

> **"Perfecting oneself is as much unlearning as it is learning."**
> **Edsgar Dijkstra[30]**

This path is as at least as much about unlearning as learning. Why? Because the search for perfection may be seen as a process of eliminating the conditioning that obscures an already present, inherent perfection. The Socratic Method is based on this notion—the premise that the questioner already has the knowledge; the seeking is simply a birthing process that brings it out. We will see in the next chapter on quality assurance that many of these principles regarding personal perfection are intertwined with process perfection through continuous improvement to eliminate the causes of defects and excessive costs.

Chapter 8

To Perfect the Outcome, Perfect the Process

> Mindfulness enables objectivity.
> When we see things as they are, we can opt to change them.

Overview

A process is the means to performance—the set of steps or actions that create a result. Every event and every result is preceded by a process. Project management and project performance are processes that occur together in the work of managing and performing a project.

This of course is classical quality management thinking, reinforced by the learning organization view best described by Peter Senge. The Zen perspective is very much in line with this thinking. Everything results from causes and conditions. There is only process, as everything is in continuous motion. By being aware of the process and being willing to make changes to it, we can control our performance.

In the previous chapter we focused on the importance of individual competency and capability as a foundation for effective performance; but even the most capable people can be brought down by inadequate processes. This chapter addresses the need to improve project performance across multiple projects over time. Its focus is on how systems thinking and a process-oriented view set the stage for effective ongoing performance improvement. We explore issues of being self observant, candid, and *compassionately ruthless* in assessing quality. We also address the causes of quality shortfalls and the subtle differences between blaming and critical analysis.

> **Candidly assess performance to identify improvement opportunities.**
> **Continuously improve the process to improve the quality of its results.**

Quality Assurance: Perfecting Performance

> "If you can't describe what you are doing as a process, you don't know what you're doing."
>
> W. Edwards Deming[31]

Quality has three facets. There is the quality of the outcome, the quality of the performance, and the quality of the process that produces the outcome. In this chapter, we address the quality of the process,[32] or Quality Assurance. The process is made up of the principles, tools, methods, structures, roles, and responsibilities that comprise the <u>way</u> the work is done.

In DeBono's Six Hats problem-solving approach, the Blue Hat is the one we put on when looking at the process itself. There is always a process. It may be consciously designed or simply allowed to develop on its own. In either case it will evolve. As it evolves, there is again the choice between conscious, intelligent design to optimize performance and just letting it evolve on its own. In the realm of business, process by design is preferred, though over-design and poor design are common. Once again, our Zen principle of balance comes into play. Balance is enabled by mindfulness and effective communication.

> **A well-designed process allows for evolution and adaptation.**

People learn and organizations learn, or fail to at their peril. Process improvement is learning. Learn from the past and you may <u>not</u> have to repeat it, unless you want to. To learn, analyze past performance. Take a systems-oriented perspective. Find and eliminate the causes of problems and expectation shortfalls, reduce the impacts of future problems, and pass on best practices for future use.

Wisdom Perspective

While we may never reach perfection, seeking it is worth the effort.

Seek balance between objectivity and subjectivity and between rigorous discipline and flexibility. Recognize the principle of cause and effect, and be compassionate while candidly criticizing performance and the process itself.

Objectively observe and then decide consciously based on the *right* degree of gut feel and objective analysis. It is unwise (if not impossible) to eliminate subjectivity. Managing and performing a project is a complex human process; the likelihood of reducing it to a formula or spreadsheet and making decisions "by the numbers" is small. It is highly skillful to look to one's "blink"[33] responses when faced with complex situations. The initial, or blink, response is quite subjective; it is influenced almost entirely by the individual's interpretation of his own experience and knowledge. It is not simply driven by the facts. Yet often we find that this first impulse is the one to follow.

Of course there are many instances in which intuitive blink responses are not effective. Malcolm Gladwell recounts an unfortunate incident in which New York City police shot and killed a man they perceived as a threat who was in fact completely innocent, cooperative, and frightened.

When there is time, and in project work there usually is, though the perception is that there isn't, the best practice is to validate intuitive knowledge with analysis. This has two benefits. One is that through analysis people can be brought into consensus about a decision that is likely to affect them. Buy-in comes out of an analysis of an idea. The second is that through analysis it is possible to avoid the pain of ineffective blink responses. The analysis consists of discussion and research to explore the reasons for the decision and its positive and negative aspects.

The statement above about there usually being enough time in projects is controversial. Many are so driven by their end dates that they fail to recognize that there is time to do it right – for example, to think and plan, to evaluate alternatives and to choose the most appropriate ones before just doing. Doing it right the first time means less chance of having to do it over. So when faced with the feeling that you must plunge ahead, ask yourself why. Will you really save time or will you trade off a long term pain for a short term benefit? Is the deadline so important that you are willing to risk quality?

Analysis need not take huge amounts of time and effort. Often all it takes is a brief reflection or a conversation among a few right people. Thinking about analysis often takes more time than doing it.

Observing

Bare awareness, seeing things as they are without embellishing them, is core to the Zen way. "When eating, just eat. When tired, just sleep"[34]

The ability to simply observe without judging is the foundation of objective critical analysis. Judging or evaluating is a next step.

> The marrow of Zen: "… your mind and body have the great power to accept things as they are, whether agreeable or disagreeable."[35]
> Shunryo Suzuki

Sometimes there is confusion about the idea of accepting things as they are. Acceptance does *not* mean having to *continue* things as they are. It means recognizing that things are the way they are, and that in that moment we cannot change them. Of course, if we take some action, or even if we don't, things probably will be different in the next moment. Part of accepting things as they are is accepting the fact that all things change and that our actions can affect that change.

Analyzing Performance—The Step After Observing

When you separate observing from judging, you can be more effective at analyzing performance. First you observe. Then you can walk the thin line between being judgmental and being discriminating. The more effective you are at analyzing performance, the more effective you are at improving.

Often we reject what we think of as being bad and focus only on the good. Zen Master Shunryo Suzuki reminds us that "One who thinks he is one of the worst husbands may be a good one if he is always trying to be a good husband with a single-hearted effort."[36] Without judgment, see things as they are. Then apply criteria to decide on the meaning of the data, whether it points to an opportunity to improve or to celebrate the perfection of the moment, or both. In this way of thinking, perfection includes the imperfections that are part of the way things are.

Judgmental implies prejudice and belief-based evaluation. *Discriminating* implies decisions based on consciously developed criteria and a clearly understood goal. If the goal is to reach increasingly higher levels of performance quality, we need a clear definition of what performance quality is and is not.

Self Observation and Mindfulness

You might ask, "What does self observation have to do with project management and quality?" Self observation enables us to see our internal process. Our internal process significantly influences the way we and the external processes we are a part of behave. Self observation is the foundation for being able to engage effectively in whatever we do.

Our internal process is a complex of thoughts, emotions, and physical sensations. It is the workings of our minds and bodies that give rise to personal behavior. Two people may react very differently to the same external conditions. For example, someone makes an error that results in some costly rework. One manager or client might respond in anger and punish or berate the one who made the error. Another, or the same one at a different time, may respond calmly and explore the cause of the error to see how it might be avoided next time. The difference has to do with the individual's internal process. Remember, every outcome whether it is a behavior or a product, is the result of a process.

Self observation is the ability to see oneself and one's process objectively. Mindfulness enables the observer to see things as they are. Mindfulness and self observation are similar but different. Mindfulness is not self focused. It is unfiltered awareness. Self observation implies a person observing him- or herself. Mindfulness is just observing. Jon Kabat-Zinn, founder of Mindfulness-Based Stress Reduction (MBSR), says "I tend to speak of it as an awareness oriented in the present moment and cultivated by paying attention on purpose with a discerning, nonjudging, nonreacting, mirror-like quality of mind which is underneath discursive thinking."[37]

Mindfulness cultivates a witnessing aspect of mind. This aspect of mind is *unobtrusively aware* of whatever is going on inside the mind as well as outside. Everyone has this witnessing mind to a degree. By consciously cultivating it, we can increase the degree to which we are mindful and bring it to the forefront of mental activity while keeping it subtle, so that it doesn't get in the way of getting things done. The witness is nonjudgmental. It is not in a leadership position.

Thoughts, emotional feelings, physical sensations, sights, sounds, and smells are objects of mindfulness. Mindfulness is a choiceless awareness that simply notes whatever is happening in the moment— seeing, thinking, feeling, hearing, smelling, tasting. Through choiceless awareness, we see our own filters, prejudices, and conditioning and can choose to do or *not* do. We replace reactivity with responsiveness. In Chapter 11 Managing From Your Center there is an instruction on how to do insight meditation, a fundamental practice for cultivating concentration and mindfulness and becoming increasingly observant of oneself while becoming increasingly aware of what is going on all around.

Mindfulness is the foundation for self awareness and self observation. Self awareness and self observation are analogous to process awareness. One is applied to the internal process, the other to the external process. The internal process of engaged individuals influences the external process, and the external process influences the internal.

Learning through Systems and Process Thinking

> "All things appear and disappear because of the concurrence of causes and conditions. Nothing ever exists entirely alone; everything is in relation to everything else."
>
> Buddha[38]

The principle of cause and effect is a one of the foundation principles of Zen. We create our future by our collective actions. Everything we observe is the result of causes and conditions. The process represents the causes and conditions that create outcomes.

This realization is key to the successful transformation of experience to learning. A learning organization improves its performance by changing its behavior to achieve the results it wants. A learning organization even goes a step further to question and, as needed, changes what it wants. Let's explore the nature of learning organizations and how they relate to performance improvement.

Peter Senge identifies five disciplines that are the core to creating a learning organization. It recognizes that reactive behavior based on old patterns is unskillful. The disciplines are:

Personal Mastery—learning to expand our personal capacity to create the results we most desire …

Mental Models—reflecting upon, continuously clarifying, and improving our internal pictures of the world, and seeing how they shape our actions and decisions

Shared Vision—building a sense of commitment in a group, by developing shared images of the future we seek to create and the principles and guiding practices by which we hope to get there

Team Learning—transforming conversations and collective thinking skills, so that a group of people can reliably develop intelligence …

Systems Thinking—a way of thinking about and a language for describing and understanding the forces and interrelationships that shape the behavior of systems ....”[39]

Senge also identifies habitual behavior (i.e., behavior that is unconscious and reactive) as a major cause of poor performance. Habitual behavior is repeating the same response over and over again even when it is not effective. It arises out of our tendency to react to events rather than cycles. Cycles are the patterns that repeat over time. They are the process repeating itself. Recognizing cycles gives us the ability to predict the future more accurately and to change it more effectively.

As an example of event-driven habitual behavior, in which we react to events, on a project that is running over budget we might react by cutting costs or admonishing the team for poor performance. When we look at the patterns that underlie the causes of the events, then we can act to change the patterns. This is a well-known principle in quality management—if there is a defect, seek its cause in the process. If you resolve the cause, the symptom goes away. So in our example, before doing anything we would explore the cause of the cost overrun. Maybe the work is running ahead of schedule and we are incurring costs that were not expected until later. Maybe the cost overrun is caused by the fact that the budget was underestimated, perhaps by someone who is not even on the project team. The right action depends on the cause and the desired outcome, not the symptom.

Once we have a sense of the cause, we can then see if there is a pattern of similar circumstances. If there is, we can explore and likely find a common or systemic cause—that is, the cause that can be eliminated to remove the root of the problem.

> "Everything should be made as simple as possible, but not simpler."
> Albert Einstein[40]

Systems Thinking

Let's focus in on systems thinking for the moment. A system is a complex of interacting entities with a boundary. The boundary is made up; it has no substance and is only a means for more effectively understanding the way things behave. Systems thinking, like Zen thinking, recognizes the intricate relationships among all things and the way that our past behavior and mental models reinforce one another to promote knee-jerk reactions. Every action has an effect. We can use systems thinking itself to describe our systems and get a better understanding of the way they operate.

Among the core principles of systems thinking are: 1) the impact of any action anywhere in the system can be felt anywhere in the system, 2) every system is embedded in a higher order system and 3) systems and parts of systems interact.

In Zen as in quality management, taking a systems and process-oriented view enables clarity and objectivity. Zen acknowledges the interrelatedness of all aspects of the process—people, things, activities, organizations, tools, and techniques. Everything is caused by something. Everything is in continuous change. Change anywhere can affect the entire system.

> Everything is a system, including the project. Every system is embedded within a higher order system.

In systems, the impact of any action can be felt throughout the system. Every system is embedded in a higher order system. Systems and parts of systems interact. A systems view enables clarity about the impact of actions. It enables us to predict how a change in one part of the system will impact the rest. Of course, the more complex the system, the less accurately we are able to predict that impact with 100 percent accuracy.

When we apply this to managing projects, we see how conditions around an individual project affect the project's performance. For example, the delay of another project or some event, like a storm or earthquake, may cause resources expected on the project to become unavailable. As estimating and scheduling is done, there is need to take a hard look at what is going on in the project environment evaluate risk, and get a realistic sense of what might happen. The chapters on expectations, estimating, risk management, and defining project objectives explore this dimension.

Process View

Commit intelligence, time, and effort to fine tune the process.

Process view recognizes that the process is the way of performing and managing the work. It acknowledges that to change the outcome, it is necessary to focus on the process. Since we tend to get lost in the content of our projects, focusing exclusively on getting things done, we often overlook *how* we get things done. The result is to unnecessarily repeat unproductive and ineffective actions. We don't learn.

"The conscious process is reflected in the imagination; the unconscious process is expressed as karma, the generation of actions divorced from thinking and alienated from feeling."
William I. Thompson[41]

"We should work on the process, not the outcome of the processes."[42]

Of course, we need to strike the right balance between process improvement and actually doing the work itself. Something like 10 percent of our attention can be devoted to process while the rest is dedicated to using the process to get things done (80 percent) and to managing them (10 percent) while they are getting done. The percentages are rough approximations. Strike your own balance based on your situation. Generally, the more room for improvement, the higher the percentage devoted to improvement efforts.

When we say 10 percent on this and 80 percent on that, we do not mean that the elements of process improvement, performance, and management can actually be discretely separated. They all occur simultaneously.

Our friend Pat applied process orientation as she convinced her staff to step back periodically to describe the way they performed their work. At first it was forced and everyone did it as a chore. But soon it became obvious that defining the way they worked led to insights that enabled them to improve.

This is another of those reminders that the ability to neatly divide things into categories, while useful, is not a true reflection of how things actually are. Process and system definitions are approximations. Boundaries, divisions and categorizations are made up to get a better understanding of the way things work. They are intellectual constructs. To maximize their usefulness, it is critically important to recognize their weaknesses.

Yet, it seems true that, as Dr. W. Edwards Deming has said, "If you can't describe what you are doing as a process, you don't know what you're doing."[43] At the same time, the ability to describe what you are doing is not a guarantee that you can do it well, or even that you really understand it.

We need to maintain a constant awareness of the process *while we are performing it.* We need to manage the process while we are performing it. As we cultivate mindfulness and the witnessing aspect of mind that it brings out, we have the experience of simultaneous awareness and performance. That gives us the ability to adjust "on the fly." Of course we also have a need to reflect on what we have done after we have done it. That is where we get the ability to learn from the past and improve our performance in the future.

The Zen way is not a simple way—it acknowledges reality, and reality is not so simple. Let go of unrealistic attempts to simplistically create an illusory process definition that looks good on paper but does not address the complex nature of systems that involve people and organizations.

Learning from the Past

In the previous chapter we addressed personal performance assessment. The same principles apply to process assessment. Learning from the past to improve the future requires ruthlessly homing in on problems and their causes. To be most effective, combine ruthlessness with compassion and understanding. The result is a *compassionate ruthlessness* that doesn't hold back from critical analysis but performs it in a way that is sensitive to the feelings of all involved.

> We may never reach perfection but we can approach it.
> What is the value of a degree of perfection? Is it worth the cost of improvement to achieve it?

The gist of the quality assurance approach discussed in this chapter is to compassionately yet ruthlessly assess performance. We recognize the needs of the people involved, including ourselves. We use the process in the quest of self-actualization and perfection of our outer form—the way we do our work. We apply objective measurement while remembering to factor in the messy subjective quality that we as humans bring to the table. We review our projects and the overall process that they are parts of.

We often learn more from mistakes than from successes, but focusing on mistakes is difficult. Resistance to criticism is common. Its source is the fear of the retribution that comes from being blamed or blaming. Some even reject the idea of admitting to performance mistakes, believing that owning up to errors makes other people lose confidence in their leadership or their performance capability.

This mental model really gets in the way of learning. An alternative model says that admission of error engenders *greater* confidence because everyone can see the error or defect anyway, and the denial or attempt at covering it up is an obvious lapse of truthfulness and objectivity. This model also says that acknowledging a defect is the first step toward correcting its cause. In Zen there is the idea that nothing is all good or all bad. Even bad things have a good quality. Errors and defects are costly, and no one really wants them. But they are facts of life, so we need to acknowledge and accept them. We extract the good from errors and defects when we use them as an opportunity to perfect the process.

Ruthless Compassion—Compassionate Ruthlessness

"Love and compassion are necessities, not luxuries. Without them humanity cannot survive."

Dalai Lama[44]

Compassion stems from recognizing ourselves in others and others in ourselves. When we realize that we are "all in it together" and have the same basic motivators and fears, we can be proactive rather than reactive. Compassion is not ordinary sympathy. It is helping others in just the right way for each individual. It is a natural attribute of our basic nature."

When we are compassionate, we do things that help, in a helpful way; we are kind and sensitive to the needs of others. We see perfecting the process as a way to serve the common good so we overcome our aversion to criticism. This is part of Peter Senge's disciplines of personal mastery, shared vision, and team learning.

To accomplish shared vision, cultivate the personal commitment to invite critical input and use it as the fuel for self improvement. We expand this commitment to team or organizational learning by agreeing as a group that continuous improvement is one of our most important behaviors.

Continuous Improvement

> "Strive for continuous improvement, instead of perfection."
> Kim Collins[45]

In the wisdom traditions we realize that perfection includes the acknowledgement of imperfection and the quality of continuous improvement. We no longer have to differentiate between perfection and continuous improvement. We accept the fact that the process is perfect in its imperfection. Continuous improvement *is* perfection.

A commitment to continuous improvement is fundamental to quality management, and quality management is fundamental to success. Continuous improvement is the highest level of process maturity.

When we look at globally accepted quality standards like ISO 9000, project management maturity models, Six Sigma, Lean, and the Software Engineering Institute's CMMI model, we find continuous improvement. A mature process may *not* be a high performing one, though if it includes a continuous improvement process, it can become one. A high performing process without continuous improvement will probably become less effective over time and miss opportunities to get even better.

Continuous improvement requires regular proactive evaluation to determine whether quality expectations are being met and/or whether they should be adjusted to improve quality. The objective is to *prevent problems* and ensure that quality improves instead of erodes over time.

> Regular self criticism and openness to critical evaluation from others are essential to success.

Continuous improvement begins with defining an improvement process. The improvement process is the way that other (target) processes will be improved. The improvement process includes measurements or key performance indicators. Performance goals (the benchmark against which performance will be evaluated) are set. The way metrics will be captured during performance, and how and when they will be reported, reviewed, and analyzed, and who will play what improvement process roles are also planned. The improvement process is further defined to identify when and how the results of performance evaluations will be transformed into action to actually improve the target process.

Effective improvement requires that the target process is accurately defined and that its performers are following the defined process, or when they are not, that they are candidly reporting the fact and the reason(s) for it.

There are many expressions of this process. A Six Sigma model is DMAIC: Define, Measure, Analyze, Improve, Control. The TQM model is PDCA: Plan, Do, Check, Act. LEAN continually squeezes waste from the process. Six Sigma analyzes defect rates and causes against a benchmark to identify opportunities for improvement. Projects are performed to take advantage of the opportunities.

In all of these models there is the need for analysis based on candid and accurate performance measurement and evaluation. In all cases, the improvement process is seen as an essential part of the target process, the process that is being continuously improved.

Of course, the improvement process itself must also be improved. After all, it is just another process. It becomes a target for itself. Like all processes, it can be imperfect. Like all processes it needs to be scaled and adapted to the needs of its environment. Sometimes measures are anecdotal. Sometimes process definitions are not complete or accurate. Sometimes baseline expectations are unrealistic. We accept the imperfections, work with and around them and seek to wring out any waste or imperfection that keeps us from optimal performance.

Performance Evaluation

Performance evaluation determines the degree to which performance meets expectations.

We have used the term **evaluation**, but **assessment** is equally used just as often.
From Merriam Webster:
Evaluate: 1: to determine or fix the value of; **2:** to determine the significance, worth, or condition of, usually by careful appraisal and study.
Assess: 1: to determine the rate or amount of (as a tax); **2a):** to impose (as a tax) according to an established rate; **b):** to subject to a tax, charge, or levy; **3:** to make an official valuation of (property) for the purposes of taxation; **4:** to determine the importance, size, or value of.

The language we use sends subtle messages. Would you rather be "evaluated" or "assessed"? Did you immediately assume evaluation or assessment come from outside—as in "audit"? How does the word *audit* make you feel? Many people report an aversion to audits, assessments, and evaluations.

As pointed out in the previous chapter on individual performance, while there is great value to external assessment, self and peer evaluation are the most powerful means for continuous improvement. We could argue that the only reason we need external audits is that we don't do self audits well enough.

Performance Measures

Performance measurement is the element that ties together the principles of nonjudgmental observation and discriminating analysis.

Measurement helps to continuously improve product quality and performance effectiveness by making sure there is a clear understanding of values and expectations. Measures identify and quantify aspects of performance so they can be compared to pre-established baselines to see if goals have been met. Baselines identify and focus attention on key performance expectations. They represent goals and values. And if the expectations are rational, they motivate higher quality performance.

If it is clear to a group of people that their performance will be measured by the degree to which they satisfy their clients, bring projects in on time, and within budget and deliver high quality products (where high quality is defined in terms of concrete criteria) it is more likely that these will be their goals. If there is a sense that it is important to just get things done on time, then that is what they will aim for.

> **Expectations may be consciously known by all parties, some parties, or not at all.**
> **Make sure they are mutually understood by everyone.**

Performance measures are of two types: 1) product quality characteristics and product performance indicators, which measure the degree to which the product meets expectations; and 2) process effectiveness indicators, which measure the quality of the process. We will focus on process quality here. Ultimately, the quality of the product (in terms of characteristics like reliability, ease of use, responsiveness, user satisfaction, cost effectiveness) is one measure of the quality of the process.

Process quality is measured in terms of success in achieving Key Performance Indicators (KPI) such as productivity, cost effectiveness, client satisfaction, on-time delivery, on-budget delivery, the consistency of product quality, continuous improvement, and performer satisfaction. The question "Does the process optimally and consistently achieve its objectives?" is asked and answered.

Identify the measures and their priorities, set the baseline, perform, measure, evaluate, decide, act, measure. Keep it up forevermore.

The measures express vision and values. Make sure they fully express the objective and subjective aspects of the desired outcome. The measures will drive performance. There is an old saying in performance measurement circles: You get what you measure. So make sure that the measures you set truly reflect what you want to accomplish. Prioritize to reflect the realities that some values are more important than others and that there will be needs for trade-offs.

> No measurement system truly reflects the "real" vision and values. Continuously improve the measures.

The baseline identifies the targets or expectations for each measure. Take care here to be realistic while "pushing the edge" to motivate excellent behavior. As we say in other chapters, setting irrational expectations creates frustration and de-motivates. Unrealistic expectations, clinging to wanting things to be different than they are, are the root causes of suffering. Continuously improve the baseline by evaluating results and seeing whether baseline metrics are setting the bar high enough or too high.

As projects are performed, measures are recorded. Project teams keep track of their hours and expenditures, project completion dates, and other metrics. This is simply a matter of observing and recording data without any filtering. Filtering or distorting the data in any way implies that either additional, unstated criteria are being applied or that the collection process is flawed. Make sure the data reflect things as they really are.

Evaluate. Analyze the data to identify successes, defects, and the patterns of behavior that underlie them. Record the results of individual project reviews and appraisals. Regularly review the process over time and across multiple projects. Use the measures to evaluate performance vis-à-vis the baseline.

Objectivity and Subjectivity

Our Zen approach is filled with paradox. Here we further explore one of the issues that often drives project managers and their clients and managers crazy—the interplay between objectivity and subjectivity.

An effective evaluation process rests on the subjective measures of stakeholder satisfaction, particularly satisfaction of clients, sponsors, and shareholders. This is a controversial issue, since subjectivity is so difficult to control and has long been a thorn in the side of people who want to improve performance.

The issue becomes clear when we reflect on the example of how an IT operations manager defended his operation against complaints of long response times from the user community. He showed them the numbers that proved that response time was very good (objectivity). They were *not* convinced since they were experiencing what they considered to be long response times (subjectivity). The numbers simply reinforced their impression of the IT people as being *idiot savants,* or at best automatons. Upon further investigation, it was found that the numbers being measured did not take into consideration communication services provided by an outside vendor. The IT manager was defending his turf by showing that his organization was doing what it was supposed to do, but failed to take into consideration the needs and perspectives of the people he was serving.

Objective measures of performance are important indicators, but they can mislead. If there are sufficient objective measures, there will be a high correlation between them and the subjective measures. If there is discord (for example, the objective measures score high but satisfaction is low) then find the objective measures that are missing. Listen to the voice of the customer and then use the numbers to diagnose short falls and show successes. Defensiveness is a waste of time and energy. Open, candid, creative cause and effect analysis based on un-filtered observation is the way to go, no matter how threatening it may be.

Both objective and subjective evaluation are needed to ensure quality. Subjective evaluation uses the powerful force of intuition and personal experience. Subjective responses are quick and based on a very complex set of interacting factors, many of which may be unconscious.

The weakness of subjective evaluation is in the fact that different people may have different views of the same thing and that those views may change randomly over time. The strength is in the fact that subjective evaluation is a truer measure of performance effectiveness, as measured by client satisfaction.

The strength of objective evaluation is in consistency; its weakness is in the tendency to evaluate based on too narrow a view.

For example, quality criteria (often set as service levels or success measures) for a project might include:

• on-time delivery
• on budget
• number of changes during project life
• number of defects in the first month of use of the product
• compliance with specifications
• measuring customer satisfaction by using a scale (e.g., 0 = terrible, 5 = excellent)

If, at a periodic review, it was found that for a large number of projects, all service levels except customer satisfaction were being met and that customer satisfaction was unacceptably low, then the reason for the disparity would be determined and both the improvement process and target process corrected.

I remember being amused at the response to this simple principle from a group of managers from the old Soviet Union. They had come to the U.S. to study quality improvement methods and I was leading a seminar that was a precursor to a set of visits to different companies around the country. When this subject of client satisfaction came up,

I gave an example of how a quality conscious hotel manager would respond to a complaint that a guest's room was not properly made up. One of the members of the group responded that in the Soviet Union the guest would be blamed for messing up the room. This type of approach inhibits complaints, and with few complaints, customer satisfaction is therefore assumed to be high by managers and reviewers.

Maybe this approach works when there are no choices; but in the competitive world we live in it is necessary to resolve the issue.

When there is a discrepancy between customer satisfaction and other criteria, likely changes to the evaluation process would be: 1) including another quality criterion (perhaps error response timeliness or the politeness of project team members); and/or 2) adjusting the service levels for any or all of the existing criteria. Likely changes to the target process would be procedural change, system enhancement, training, among others.

Commonly, one measure or metric is prioritized to the exclusion of all other criteria of performance (for example, project completion on schedule, or computer-time efficiency). Performers may be motivated to achieve the objective represented by the metric, even though other criteria may be more critical to the organization over time (e.g., user friendliness, reliability, flexibility). To avoid this, work with several metrics that are combined to create an index of performance. Make sure that both short term and long-term needs are addressed

Metrics are an aid for use in evaluation, not a replacement for intuitive evaluation and good sense. Don't stop thinking.

Banish Fear

The Zen approach recognizes the continuous interplay between intrapersonal thoughts and emotions and people's behavior in the interpersonal space. In other words, the way we think and feel drives our behavior and our behavior affects those around us and ourselves. Also, the things happening around us impact the way we think and feel. Being aware of this interplay enables responsive rather than reactive behavior. We can choose.

Performance improvement requires that resistance to critical evaluation be resolved. There is need to carefully engineer measurement and evaluation to clearly identify and regularly reinforce the concept that performance measurement and evaluation are done to improve future performance, not to punish people for making errors or otherwise not performing to expectations.

As Dr. Deming advises, "Banish fear." Among the issues commonly raised by project performers is the lack of knowledge regarding what is being done with performance measures. Tell them and invite feedback. Performers may simply *work for the numbers,* rather than for overall process quality, unless it is clear that the goal is overall performance excellence.

Dr. Deming's 90-10 Rule states that 90 percent of all defects have systemic causes and, only 10 percent are directly caused by individual performance. Blaming and punishing an individual not only de-motivates, it avoids the real problem and increases the likelihood that the defect will occur again and again.

> **Blaming is worthless. It makes performance analysis impossible.**

The Paradox of Personal Performance and Systemic Causes

Unfortunately, it is common to find that there is a hunt for guilty parties as opposed to a hunt for systemic causes. This, of course, perpetuates problems and drives everyone away from <u>real</u> critical analysis and process improvement. Linked to this tendency to blame individuals for performance problems is exhorting people to work harder and smarter.

Who but a Zen PM would argue with asking people to be more careful, take personal responsibility to reduce errors and save money. Of course we want each individual to work harder and smarter. However, it is necessary to mention systemic causes. Not doing so takes the attention away from the most probable causes of errors—flaws in the system – and may instill fear of being blamed. Here is another instance of Zen balance. Not a total focus on individual responsibility for performance that can easily shift into blame and recrimination—"you made a mistake." Instead a focus on both individual responsibility and on addressing the systemic causes of errors and omissions.

Systemic causes are flaws in the process that result in errors. To improve performance, address the work *system* as well as the individual worker. Deming once commented, "It is a mistake to assume that if everybody does his job, it will be all right. The whole system may be in trouble."[47]

> Put a good performer into a bad system and the system will win. The mediocre will stay and adapt to the bad system. The excellent will leave.

Among the attributes of excellent individual behavior is taking responsibility for speaking out regarding process flaws. Excellent systems invite such criticism and institutionalize continuous improvement. Focus attention on cause removal. Seek the root causes, not just the symptoms.

In the tenth of his fourteen points, Dr. Deming advised to "Eliminate slogans, exhortation, and targets for the workplace." Exhortation linked to slogans, which may be true enough and motivational, miss the point. They often leave the impression that individuals, working on their own, are responsible for avoiding problems that are most likely linked to systemic causes like inadequate procedures, lack of clear understanding of ownership, accountability and responsibility, inadequate training, and overwork, among others.

Project and Process Reviews

Reviews are the means for assessment. In project work there are two types that address performance: process reviews, and project reviews.

In both project and process reviews, be both objective and sensitive to the tendency to avoid negative criticism. The acknowledgement of failure or poor performance is difficult. It is particularly difficult when there are restrictions to doing the cause and effect analysis that is critical to improvement efforts. If some causes are off limits, the sense that the whole review process is a political game is reinforced. For example, imagine a situation in which everyone knows in his or her heart that the cause of schedule overruns is the insistence by senior management to stick to irrational deadlines and that it is impossible to raise and address the issue because middle management won't allow it for fear that they will be punished by the senior managers for the criticism of their decisions. How likely is it that the organization will learn? How will the most effective performers feel and what might they do?

Mindful Dialogue

Mindful dialogue is the use of communication as opportunity for mindfulness and concentration practice. During any conversation or meeting, make the intention to stay with the content as a point of attention. Notice thoughts, feelings, physical sensations, sounds, sights, smells, and bring the attention back to the moment at hand and the communication. Project and process reviews are prime practice opportunities.

Remember our old friend Pat? She reported that in a recent review she attended she applied this practice. She clearly saw how she personally reacted when a work product she felt responsible for was criticized by two of the four other participants.

She reported that "The sensations in my lower abdomen were rising into a tightening in my chest and throat. I felt, saw, and heard myself begin to become defensive, even before the critic finished her comments. I was able to pull back—it took a great effort—listen, and reflect. As the other proponents of the product had their say, I was able to moderate the defensiveness. I found myself highlighting and acknowledging the points that were made by the critical participant.

"It was only after that that we as group were able to explore the issues and their causes without being encumbered by our emotional reactions."

Project Reviews

Project reviews focus on the performance of a single project. They are best performed by the project's stakeholders and facilitated by an objective person who assembles information by interviewing individuals and reviewing project records. The facilitator guides the participants through discussion of the way the project was performed and how it could have been better performed. Analysis is done to identify the causes of defects and problems and to identify best practices that may be useful in future projects. Flaws in the process are highlighted.

A typical project review checklist consists of questions to address client satisfaction; the degree to which project time, cost, and quality objectives have been met, the effectiveness of project management and performance tools and techniques, the degree to which organizational structures supported the project, and perhaps most importantly, the health of interpersonal relationships. Changes, defects, and issues that arose during the project are principle inputs to the process.

Results of project reviews should be published no matter how embarrassing they are to the project stakeholders. These results are the principle input to process reviews.

> The best way to guarantee continuous poor performance is to hide the latest instance of it.

Process Reviews

While project reviews focus on a single project, process reviews look at multiple projects across time. Project reviews are performed to identify *lessons learned* through an analysis of the problems and issues encountered in the specific project being reviewed. Process reviews identify trends and evaluate lessons learned from many projects to identify opportunities for improvements to the way projects are managed and performed. Project reviews provide a primary input to process reviews. Additional input to PM process reviews comes from an analysis of the portfolio management process (the way projects are selected and authorized) and the experience and emerging needs of functional managers, project performers, and clients.

Process reviews focus on performance in a number of projects. They determine 1) if the process is meeting quality criteria; 2) if the quality criteria are adequate; and 3) if the quality is improving, based on trend analysis. Assess process quality regularly.

Generally, because they deal with data collected across multiple projects and because the reviews are a step removed from the evaluation of direct performance, process reviews are less emotionally charged than project reviews. That doesn't mean there is *no* emotional component. For example, the quality of the process definition and the level of compliance to it are very often the subject of conflict among a number of parties in the management of projects. Performers might say that if they had more autonomy to decide how to operate, they would perform better. Those who define the process may insist, even in the face of evidence to the contrary, that the defined process is perfect.

Process reviews are performed by process owners. Process owners may or may not be active project managers. If they are not, then they must be sure to remember that they represent project managers. Process owners are *not* owners in the normal sense of the word. They are custodians of the process. Their job is to ensure that the process used in projects is as effective as possible. They identify opportunities and promote action to improve the process. They serve process users. They should not be policing them, or behaving like rigid bureaucrats. They may use Six Sigma, Lean, or other quality management methods.

Often process custodians, usually members of a Project Management Office (PMO) or Center of Excellence (COE), have been project managers but no longer actually manage projects. If they lose touch with the real world as it is experienced by the people currently managing and performing projects, they may make things worse instead of better. It is critical that the process custodians involve the principle performers in decisions to improve the process. Each improvement is a change that affects the way people work. Manage the change by communicating the reason for it, obtaining buy-in, and being open to critical feedback regarding its effectiveness.

Taking Action—Cause Removal

> Problems do not spontaneously generate nor do they spontaneously pass away.

Reviews without action are a waste of time and energy; worse, they demotivate. Follow reviews with improvements to the target process, to the measurements being used, and to the evaluation process itself. If no action is to be taken, say so and say why.

As we keep saying, everything has a cause. That is why the fundamental approach to process improvement is cause analysis followed by cause removal. Reviews identify problems (performance shortfalls) as well as best practices. While it is important to identify best practices and carry them forward as process improvements, it is most likely that the greatest value for performance improvement is from the analysis of problems and issues.

This goes back to the Zen principle of finding the beneficial aspect of anything that presents itself. If a disturbing thought or behavior arises, greet it as you would an old friend. Convert its energy into a positive channel. Grow from it.

Nothing Is Sacred

For improvement to be as successful as possible there must be freedom to address causes and get down to the root causes. Frequently, this leads to the policy and procedures associated with the highest echelons of organizations.

If projects are late, a common cause is the initiation of too many projects for the staff to handle. This, coupled with frequent priority shifts, causes resources to be shifted from project to project, and that causes schedules to slip, among other problems.

In this instance, the broken process is the priority-setting project initiation part of the portfolio management process. This process is owned by a planning group or PMO and operated by senior managers and executives. Is it subject to critical analysis? Is it clearly recognized as a business process? Do executives promote (not just allow) their processes and the decisions that result to be critically analyzed as part of the cause analysis? If not, there is little chance of a lasting solution.

The old story about Nasruddin, the Sufi wise man/fool, points to the all too common attempt to apply solutions where it is easy to apply them, instead of where it is probable that they will make a difference. Nasruddin is looking for his lost key under the street lamp instead of by the door where he dropped it. When asked why? Nasruddin answered "Because it is dark over by the door. How could anyone find anything there?"

In the search for meaningful and lasting solutions, nothing is sacred except the notion that an essential foundation for quality is objective critical analysis that seeks root causes and acts upon them. The objectives of quality reviews are to determine if 1) the product is meeting quality criteria; 2) if the quality criteria are adequate; and 3) if the quality is improving (based on trend analysis of service levels).

Recap

Continuous improvement is made up of a combination of radical and incremental change efforts that come out of critical performance evaluation.

To be successful, be candid, objective, and system and process oriented. Rely on well-planned measurements against realistic benchmarks. Make sure that everyone understands the real goals of the target process and of continuous improvement. Remember that the ultimate goal is satisfying the needs of clients, sponsors, shareholders, and other stakeholders, including project performers. Assess the effectiveness of objective measures by correlating them with satisfaction survey results.

The interpersonal factors in continuous process improvement are the most critical of all. Banish fear and blaming. Stop posting slogans exhorting people to be better performers. A compassionate, candid, and laser-like focus on squeezing out waste and eliminating the causes of defects and deficiencies is the most effective way to continuously improve. At the same time there is need, on the personal level, to get past the self-defeating behavior of criticism avoidance.

The Zen practitioner is ruthless and compassionate. Ruthless in the continuous effort to approach perfection—his own as well as the perfection of the process he is part of. Compassionate in the recognition of peoples' sensitivity.

The Zen practitioner sees the universe as a complex of systems and processes. She knows that all things are the result of causes and conditions in any process. She also knows that in order to assess anything as complex as quality there has to be a balance between subjectivity and objectivity.

Chapter 9

The Balance Between Structure and Flexibility

There's some ancient wisdom about how to keep horses.

If you put a horse in a tight pen either it will kick its way out or become too docile.

If you keep the horse in an open, unfenced area it will wander away.

If you keep a horse in an area that gives it enough space to exercise and have a sense of freedom, it will be satisfied. When it reaches the fence it will turn and go in a different direction because it is not worth the effort to jump the fence.

Overview

This chapter is a natural extension of the previous chapter on process quality. It explores agility, discipline, defined process, and formality. These are left-brain, analytical activities. They are in balance with the right brain qualities of creativity, adaptability, and sensitivity.

The optimum integration of these qualities enables performance excellence with minimal bureaucracy and overhead while supporting control, strategic planning, and continuous improvement. Conditions like project size, complexity and criticality, legal issues, and the team's composition, among others are parameters used to drive how much formality and control are necessary.

In the previous chapter on process quality we said that *defined pro-*

cess is a foundation for improvement. But, with or without a defined process, there is a 'right' degree of rigor and discipline based on the needs of the project and its environment.

This chapter addresses an aspect of project management that is often the realm of methodologists and architects. The content is meant to be of interest to both the methodologists and architects who define the process and the people who live with it.

Zen of Process

When we address process issues we take a step back from the microscopic, day to day, operational performance of the process. We look from a different perspective, observing the process. What is that perspective? Is there greater clarity? We can see our own process and appreciate the power that just seeing it gives us to perform optimally.

The inner work here is to apply the principles to your personal self-actualization. The outer work is to enable stellar performance.

From a Zen perspective, how can we rest in the right dynamic balance between them, as the star performer rests in his performance? Mindfulness, conscious awareness, and concentration are the methods.

Earlier in the book we defined a process as a set of activities to accomplish something; a means to an end. Anytime there is a result, a process produced it. A process may be defined in writing or not defined at all. Its performers may be more or less conscious of their process.

Defined Process and Consciousness

While there are pros and cons to defining processes, few argue for less consciousness.

Process consciousness means having a sense of the discrete activities and their effects as they are being performed. Consciousness of our actions and their consequences is a prerequisite for adaptability and continuous improvement. Mindfulness is the means for being increasingly conscious of the process.

There is always a process, and it is the key to performance. Knowing this, when we focus attention on the process, we are able to analyze it, squeeze out waste, and fine tune it over time. We addressed this in the last chapter. Here we take a look at the attributes of effective processes.

Defined Process

A defined process is one that has been described in words and/or pictures. It describes what to do, maps roles to activities, and may also include instruction on how to do perform them. It identifies and defines inputs, tools, techniques, and outputs for each activity or step, describes decision points and criteria, and identifies activity timing and frequency. For each step, input, output, tool, and technique there may be a tutorial, best practice, or procedure.

> No complex human process can be fully described. The description is an approximation that is never the same as the process itself.

Defining a process is useful if the definition is true to the actual process. The truly effective description acknowledges its limitations. It defines where the performers' expertise must come into play to make appropriate decisions to address the needs of their situation.

Projects are complex, involving interpersonal relationships, organizations, significant costs, and sensitive situations. Complex processes do not lend themselves to simple straightforward definitions. An effective definition must address process subtleties and provide appropriate space for flexibility and creative adaptation. The more complex the process, the greater the need for expertise and flexibility.

The principle disadvantage of defined process is the tendency for people to follow the "book" even when the book is an incomplete or inaccurate picture of what really needs to be done. Instead of creatively adapting to the needs of the moment, people will overly rely on a procedures manual to tell them what to do next. While this may have its place in some cases, it is not appropriate for most project management work.

Lao Tse the Taoist philosopher, is said to have ordered his disciples <u>not</u> to write down his teachings. He felt that once written they would be followed as beliefs and taken out of context. He wanted people to think, feel, and act spontaneously in the moment.

Of course, the "pros" of defined process are compelling. Definition enables different people to do the same thing in more or less the same way and this makes transferring knowledge about best practices and moving people between projects easier. It also makes clients who may be involved in multiple projects more comfortable and confident. Process definition is the foundation for continuous improvement; it enables critical analysis among many performers. It makes "reinventing the wheel" unnecessary and saves time and money. Why come up with a new way of doing something when there is a good, proven, standard way to do it? Defined process also reduces the need for as many super performers who can operate in uncharted territory by making it possible for good performers to operate on a higher level than they could if the process were not defined.

How do we manage the conflict between these pros and cons? The wise PM seeks a process description that clearly communicates that there is no cookbook. Instead there are frameworks, guidelines, best practices, "musts," typical activities, typical relationships, tools, and other ingredients that can be combined to address the needs of a situation.

The defined process is a *starting point* for the process to be applied in a specific project. The project specific process, defined at the start of the project, is subject to flexible application during the course of the project, as things change.

Project Management and Performance Methodologies

A project consists of performance and management activities.

A project management (PM) methodology is the defined process for the project management activities. The PM methodology addresses the activities, sequence, roles, relationships, inputs and outputs, techniques, and tools to *manage* a project. A performance methodology addresses the way a project is to be *performed*. For example, the steps to create a website or to build a small house; while they can be managed similarly, must be performed very differently.

The word *methodology* is off- putting to many. It is so formal and technical. It has five (5) syllables! Synonyms for methodology are method, procedure, process, technique, approach, and means. The Brainy Dictionary[48] defines a *method* as "an orderly procedure or process; regular manner of doing anything hence, manner; way; mode; as, a method of teaching languages; a method of improving the mind; Orderly arrangement, elucidation, development, or classification; clear and lucid exhibition; systematic arrangement peculiar to an individual."

Method and methodology are not quite the same, though. The *ology* in methodology implies a studied writing; a science. A project management methodology defines the method for many projects. Its leveraged impact on overall performance is significant.

Many organizations prefer to call their PM methodology a *framework,* a word that more effectively communicates the open, flexible quality that promotes creative adaptation. Others simply refer to theirs as a process or as procedures. A "rose by any other name would smell as sweet"—or would it?

Discipline, Rigor—Yikes!

This chapter begins with the *Horses* analogy—to keep it available, active, and healthy, pen a horse in a space that is neither too tight nor too open. If the rules are too rigid, there won't be enough room for the flexibility people need to succeed. If the rules are always applied in the same way, then there will be either too much paperwork and bureaucracy or not enough. If the rules are too loose, there is inefficiency and avoidable risk.

PM may be done more or less formally. Finding the right balance is necessary to avoid unnecessary work and to make sure the project is effectively initiated, planned, controlled, executed, and closed.

Formal means putting project understandings (e.g., plans, decisions, objectives, requirements, definitions, change requests) in writing, clearly defining roles and responsibilities to promote accountability and ultimately following a pre-established, repeatable process. Formality implies disciplined use of practices that add value. Discipline is most effective when it is self-imposed and when there is acceptance that following the discipline pays off.

Formality without flexibility leads to bureaucracy. Bureaucracy is too costly and too slow for today's fast moving, fast changing world. Flexibility without formality, and the structure it brings, is chaos. Chaos is also too costly and inappropriate given the complexity and impact of projects.

Picture the novice skier who is too impatient to take lessons and gets right out on the slope going really fast and unable to stop or turn. Chaos. Picture the expert, in control, yet fluid and fast.

Picture the client who gets a bill that is four times what she expected because she made hundreds of small changes during the project and was in too much of a hurry to take the time to get cost estimates for each. Do you think she would be happy? While she would probably complain about the "annoying" process of staying in control, she would probably be much happier in the end if she made informed decisions.

Balance

What is the right balance? The right balance depends on the needs of the situation.

For a project being performed in a regulated industry like pharmaceuticals it is necessary to follow procedures very closely. Rigor and discipline are imposed by law. Failure to comply results in significant penalties. One pharmaceutical firm was barred from selling its products until its methodology was defined and auditable. The cost was tens of millions.

In redoing the kitchen or in an internal IT setting there may be no legal requirement to follow a methodology. But, discipline and rigor can nevertheless be mandated internally to avoid preventable error and to promote performance consistency and better results and services.

In small projects, performed once every several years, like moving an office, the degree of discipline depends on the skill and experience of the performers and on the degree to which they are willing and able to accept the risk that comes along with working ad hoc. In this kind of project, discipline would address contracts with vendors, written schedules, a change control process, and checklists of all the tasks to be performed. The standard process may come in the form of a previous plan rather than a corporate standard.

In large projects, costs and potential risks dictate the need for a disciplined approach.

Tuning the instrument

What are the risks of *not* being formal enough? The risk that when you agreed to a price with a handshake, maybe you were thinking "fixed fee" and the other guy was thinking "ballpark estimate" for a price based on charges for time and materials. Or, the risk that some participants will have different ideas about deadlines, content, quality, and their roles and responsibilities. Or, the risk that there are will be no phones on move-in day.

The Buddha spoke of tuning a stringed instrument. Too tight and the string breaks, too loose and there is no music. Our processes are instruments that need to be tuned for optimum performance. We create the dynamic balance that makes our music.

Working Lean and Agile

Agility is the ability to move with speed and grace; to be nimble. "Lean," the quality program, seeks to squeeze waste out of every process—to do only what is necessary.

What is the minimal activity to get the job done well? When we can answer that question we have the base for a Lean and agile PM process—a process that is quick and graceful because it has no excess and one that does what it is designed to do because there is no insufficiency.

> Formality and agility are two different things.
> Formality does not preclude agility.
> We need to be both formal and agile. Just agile isn't enough.
> Formality gives structure and direction to agility.
> Too much formality and we have excessive overhead and performance barriers.

The Agile Alliance (http://www.agilealliance.org) has a Manifesto for Agile Software Development which we can apply to project management. As it is written, though, there may be a tendency to promote division rather than consensus. Let's explore the manifesto in light of a Zen-like balance. The manifesto says:

"We are uncovering better ways of developing software by doing it and helping others do it. Through this work we have come to value:

Individuals and interactions over processes and tools

Working software over comprehensive documentation

Customer collaboration over contract negotiation

Responding to change over following a plan.

That is, while there is value in the items on the right, we value the items on the left more."

The Zen approach seeks dynamic balance. Even though the last sentence in the manifesto tries to bring out a need for balance, some tend to think in absolutes and are apt to throw the baby out with the bathwater.

How much more valuable are the preferred items (individuals and interactions, working products, customer collaboration, and responding to change)—than the others (process and tools, comprehensive documentation, contract negotiation, and following a plan)?

In Zen we look at the total picture and do <u>not</u> get lost in conflicts. The big picture view turns conflicts into resolutions. First we recognize a continuum between left and right. They are parts of a unified whole. Then, we add some criteria to make it easier to maintain balance within the continuum. The next few paragraphs are my summary of the Agile Manifesto's principles and exploration of how it can be reconstituted using the Zen approach.

Individuals and Interactions
Using Processes and Tools

Process and tools are means for enhancing the effectiveness of individuals and interactions. The process and tools must be flexible with the minimum amount of overhead and restrictiveness to satisfy the need for control and consistency. Individuals must be empowered to creatively adapt, within appropriate constraints. They must be motivated to communicate and collaborate. For example, a process for naming and controlling documents combined with a tool for document management and collaboration support would make individual effort and interaction more effective.

Allowing everyone to do their own thing leads to confusion, unnecessary rework, and conflict.

Working Products and the Right Degree
of Comprehensive Documentation

If "comprehensive" means all the documentation that is needed, then why value it less than the product itself? Software is an example. We could be talking about any product. A working product is often useless without comprehensive documentation. Consider the pharmaceutical company that had good working product but could not sell it because there was insufficient documentation to satisfy the government regulators and the needs of its sales people, dispensers, and users.

Of course, documentation without the product is probably more likely to be useless than the product without documentation. I can't think of anyone who wants the documentation for how to work a new appliance without the appliance. In reality, we need the working product itself *and* its documentation.

Project management documentation is in addition to product documentation. It is often harder to justify. It includes plans, status reports, change requests, issues, and contracts. Maybe it isn't as valuable as the product and its documentation, but PM documentation is valuable. It is a means for controlling and communicating within the project and for providing the basis for learning from the project in order to improve the process. In the last chapter we highlighted the value of project and process reviews. PM documentation enables objective reviews.

Of course, having more documentation than is necessary to satisfy needs is simply *not* clever. Documentation is costly in time and money. It has to be managed and maintained. Why spend more than is needed? The goal is to deliver the *right* documentation. Not too little. Not too much. If a simple e-mail is enough to document an agreement, there is no need for a complex document in legalese.

Customer Collaboration Through Contract Negotiation

As for customer collaboration and contract negotiation, aren't they one and the same thing? Whenever we collaborate with a customer we are creating a contract—implied or explicit; legally binding or not. The contract (you may call it an understanding, agreement, service level agreement, letter of understanding, or whatever you like) states the expectations that bind the parties.

"Good fences make for good neighbors."[49]

If negotiation becomes divisive, then get better at negotiating. In project management as elsewhere, win-win results both support greater collaboration and result from collaboration and negotiation. The absence of written understandings and rigid adherence to the letter rather than the spirit of the contract detract from collaboration and lead to unnecessary conflict.

Responding to Change While Following a Plan

Can we follow a plan *and* respond to change? Of course we can. In fact, following a well-crafted plan makes responding to change easier and more effective. It may also reduce the number of changes to respond to. But, it is realistic to be concerned about blindly following a plan. Blindly following a plan will make responding to change more difficult or unlikely. If the PM thinks following a plan means doing whatever the plan says without evaluating it in light of the present situation and never changing the plan; that is a problem.

The plan, like a defined process, represents a baseline and a starting point. Effective PMs recognize this and plan for change, enable positive change, and inhibit unnecessary change. Positive change is change that is needed to meet project and objectives in the face of progressive elaboration and understanding of those needs, changes in the marketplace, availability of resources, and other aspects of the project environment.

Too much detail in the plan is as bad as too little. Not taking the time to assess and plan for risk is just asking for trouble.

These last two sentences may seem contradictory to some. In the Zen and in fact all wisdom approaches we constantly come back to the principle of balance. Not this way; not that way, but somewhere in between. The right balance depends on the needs of each situation.

The Need for Control

Software is only one of many industries in which "extremists" make absolute statements that guarantee misunderstanding and conflict. There is a need for control and for consciously attempting to influence the future.

The Agile and X (Extreme) methods have downplayed the need to control costs and schedules. Their promoters have the idea that clients cannot know the outcomes of projects until the project is over. Of course, in an absolute sense no one can know the outcome of a project until it is over. But, it is certainly possible and reasonable for a client to have a reliable sense of what she is going to get for her money.

Maybe she can't know *exactly* what she will get but she should have a pretty good sense of it before she lays out the money. Sure, there are no guarantees, but for my money I want a pretty solid idea of the expected outcome and an update every so often about what I will really be getting, for how much, and when I will be getting it. While I may not be able to predict the future with 100 percent accuracy, I should be able to approximate it.

The Agile Alliance says, "Build projects around motivated individuals. Give them the environment and support they need, and trust them to get the job done." Sounds good. But it does not tell us how to control costs and schedule.[50] Nor does it tell us what to do about the wide variety of skill levels, work ethics, and motivation among the people available to perform the work.

While trust is very important and worthwhile, not everyone is trustworthy. Trust is built on experience. Without experience, trust is wishful thinking. In many projects, trust just isn't enough to satisfy the need for control.

Have the people done it before? Have they done it well? Do they have personal integrity? Are they ethical? Are they adaptive and creative or more likely to follow a prescribed path, no matter what? Do they tend to act like two-year-olds, adolescents, or adults? What are their

Emotional and Intelligence Quotients? These are some of the questions that come to mind when I think about whether I can trust a person or team.

In PM, as in life, trust is balanced by continuous evaluation of current performance. In the Agile Alliance's stance "Give them the environment and support they need, and trust them to get the job done," does environment and support include controls, accountability, and leadership? If it does, then we can trust the people to get the job done. If not, then we'd better think twice about it.

Create the right degree of space. Not too tight. Not too loose.

The Bottom Line: Are Business and Client Needs Met?

In the end, the measure of success of the process is whether stakeholder needs are met. Client needs include quality, delivery time, and cost as well as minimal disruption. Business (sponsor, shareholder) needs include regulatory compliance, healthy customer relationships, risk management, cost control, profitability, and alignment of multiple projects and programs with strategy. Performer needs include reasonable working environments and the ability to "have a life" outside of work, to grow and feel appreciated.

There is no cookbook, but there are defined processes that are cleverly engineered and can be used to rightly balance flexibility and discipline to enable truly agile and effective project management.

Compliance

Are you awake?

Once a group of people agree on a defined process, they may use it for a single project or across many. The defined process for a single project is the project's plan, which includes the procedures and tools to be used in its performance and management.

Compliance monitoring is another one of those really formal sounding and bureaucracy inducing terms. It is a synonym for audit. Compliance monitoring imposes discipline to make sure that people are performing according to the way they said they would perform.

Does that bring up any emotional charge? Is there resistance regarding compliance monitoring? It is so police-state-ish to some; fear- or anger-producing for others.

In general, it is best that those who perform the work monitor their own compliance with process standards and the project plan. They periodically put on their compliance monitor hats and see if they are following the plan and process they set out to follow. If *not,* they may choose to continue as they are going or return to their "baseline" process. Either way they should be conscious of why they are out of compliance. The more conscious they are about the reasons for this, and the more they communicate it, the more easily the process definition can be fine tuned to better mirror the real process.

The PM project manager and her manager, client, and sponsor have a vested interest in compliance to the defined process. The PM and her manager are accountable to the others as well as to regulators and auditors for the degree of compliance agreed to for the project. The client and sponsor must pay for any shortfalls that result from cutting corners, working "seat-of-the-pants," and taking unnecessary risks.

Because it is so easy to "get lost in the doing," it is often necessary to have someone from outside the project get people to pick up their heads and see where they are from a process point of view. External process compliance is common in regulated, corporate, and institutional settings.

Compliance can be monitored during the project or after its completion as part of post-project review. When a project has checkpoints, one of the key issues to be addressed is whether the *right* documents have been delivered to the decision makers. The presence of acceptable documents is the evidence that the process has been followed, at least to the degree that the documents are accurate. Documents like the project budget and schedule, contracts, progress information, and decision packages, if they meet acceptance criteria, are proof that the project is being managed according to the agreed upon process. Deciding if the documents are acceptable is both quality control and compliance monitoring.

External compliance monitors must be knowledgeable about the process, both as it is described (the *de jure* process) and how as it is performed in the real-world (the *de facto* process). They must understand and communicate what their aims are and why the aims are important. They must seek reasons for noncompliance and be willing to grant variances when they are justified.

Avoid the Compliance Police

In the Zen, Yogic, and Taoist views, everything has a shadow side. Again, it is the dynamic balance.

The danger of external compliance monitoring is its tendency to become rigid and to elicit fear of stepping outside the box. Creativity may suffer. Bureaucratic conflicts and waste may be too high a price to pay for conformance. Note that given the need to choose, performance is more important than compliance. However, as noted earlier, there are exceptions when compliance is imposed by law.

There is often a serious divide between performers and monitors. The PMs view their job as getting the project done on schedule and budget. They may see compliance monitoring as something that is in the way—a useless extra. Monitors may add to the problem by being rigid and insensitive. The compliance monitoring approach, if it does <u>not</u> put enough reliance on self-monitoring during project life, can make things worse.

It is best if process expectations are clearly understood from the beginning of the project. Then the PM and performers feel motivated to comply because they understand both the need and their accountability, and will integrate compliance monitoring into the project's quality control process.

In the end, if the defined process can be relied upon to deliver good results, most people will follow it. More will follow it if they know *why* the process is the way it is and why following it is important. Still more will follow it if they know that they will be accountable for <u>not</u> following it and if they are confident that it can be improved for future projects.

> "Even though its technique appears poor and unrefined, it is the unshaken mind that is the master one can rely on." Kamiizumi-isenokam1 (1508-?), founder of the Shinkage School of swordsmanship[51]

In Zen there are no rigid rules. There are skillful means like right speech, livelihood and action. These are skillful because they promote wisdom and compassion. The practitioner follows because following adds value. The unshaken mind is the mind that can concentrate and rest in the moment, un-phased by the whirlwind of activities around it.

Variance and Flexibility

Variance is another daunting word. It is an essential ingredient in defined and compliance monitored process. It is the antidote to rigidity. A variance is permission to *not* follow the standard process. In formal settings, a PM goes to the compliance monitors in advance of the project and requests permission to change the process. Here is an opportunity to apply flexibility and to incrementally improve the process over time.

If a variance is justified and there is a pattern—every time you do one of these projects you do it this way, even though the standard process says do it some other way—then when conditions are right you change the process to include the better way of doing things. Build a library of variations mapped to project characteristics like size and type. The more variations that are built into the defined process, the fewer variances and the greater the usefulness of the definition.

Recap

The theme of this chapter was to consciously engineer your process so that it is excellent. Doing this means finding the right dynamic balance among agility, discipline, defined process, and formality. Through the dynamic balance among these, success and performance excellence are more likely.

With or without a formal methodology, the PM must apply the degree of disciplined formality needed to satisfy situational needs for regulatory compliance and due diligence. At the same time, the PM should seek to apply an agile or lean approach. This means the minimal amount of discipline and documentation to satisfy needs, including the needs of regulators, process custodians, and project stakeholders.

Nothing in excess. No insufficiency.

Finally, the awareness of one level of process and the ability to detach from the day to day view to engineer the process opens the practitioner to exploring all levels of process. We are in a highly complex matrix of processes. Every result is the outcome of a process. Psychological, physical, emotional, and spiritual processes intersect and merge together.

How awake are you to the levels of process operating in and around you?

Going Beyond the Intellect

In Zen there is the need to go beyond the intellect. Consider the following from Dogen Zenji:

"To study the way is to learn the self. To study the self is to forget the self. To forget the self is to be enlightened by all things. To be enlightened by all things is to remove barriers between one's self and others."[52]

The next two chapters will address two major aspects of the process—the collaborative effort required on teams and more about the inner process and its ways.

Chapter 10

Working in Teams

> **The best teamwork comes from men who are working indepen-dently toward one goal in unison.**
>
> **James Cash Penney[53]**

Overview

"The single most important factor in maximizing the excellence of a group's product was the degree to which the members were able to create a state of internal harmony, which lets them take advantage of the full talent of their members.[54]"

From the Wisdom perspective, the foundation for effective teamwork and all relationships is an attitude of compassion and loving kindness that stems from the recognition that we are all in it together —we all have the same basic condition. This attitude is supported by mindfulness. In Zen the true master chooses to devote all of his efforts to help others become free of their suffering. The Sanskrit term for this is Bodhisattva. What would our teams and other relationships be like if we took this attitude? A lovely concept!

People and the way they join together to work in teams are the most exciting, essential and complex elements in project work. This chapter explores what teams are and how they can be managed to maximize the effectiveness of every member while creating a stimulating, joyful, supportive environment. In earlier chapters we have discussed individual performance and work process. These come together when teams perform the work needed to satisfy the expectations set through estimating, risk management and scope definition.

Exercise: Exploring the Cause of Emotions

When better to do the inner work of self-actualization than in the context of relationships. Teamwork is all about relationships and relationships are filled with challenges. The practitioner who wants to free himself from being reactive and wants to truly join his team in the most effective way can take on an exercise. Instead of blaming external conditions, like the behavior of others, for your emotions, do an exercise to explore how your perspective causes your emotions.. The external behavior is a trigger but the emotion and all that follows it are created internally. When we mindfully explore this and stay with our emotions without either suppressing or fueling them we increasingly bring our conditioned responses to conscious awareness. We add to this the intention to do no harm and in fact help as we can, and we can be a real team player.

> In India it is common to greet another by placing the hands together in the center of the chest, bowing slightly and saying "Namaste"— I greet that part of ourselves we share, our essential nature.

In the Wisdom ways the common understanding is that we can see one another more clearly when we merge our subjectivity -- meaning that if we remember our unity with the other we can more effectively work together in the relative world where our differences are real. Here is another paradox: we are one in essence but we are also individuals with all that that brings to relationship.

So the next part of the exercise is to explore the concept that the root cause of these relationship issues is the habitual tendency to view others as others and ourselves as ourselves.

Serve and Respect Everyone: An Example

Short of being able to merge and remember that we are essentially one (a difficult thing to do given the years of conditioning that reinforces the sense that we are different and distinct from one another) we cultivate respect for everyone else and for ourselves.

In a recent project it became clear that an influential team member was operating in a way that made others on the team feel that they were being disrespected. She made unilateral decisions without regard to the way they impacted other peoples' schedule commitments and barely communicated about issues that impacted a number of team members. She tended to leave her editing and review work to the last minute, thereby putting pressure on others who had to squeeze their work in, usually in overtime efforts.

When confronted with the pattern of behavior, there was always a good reason for doing it—a new client contact or pressure to meet with the boss ate up her time and the project tasks she committed to slipped.

So how does this relate to respect? If there is respect for one's teammates and for oneself as well, the individual does not take the easy way out. The easy way is to prioritize work for clients and bosses and let the work required to support one's peers and subordinates slip to the back burner. Saying "no" or "later" to the client or boss is an option. Mostly, people understand and are somewhat flexible, though the attachment to getting new business and being in the good graces of the boss often makes this option unacceptable. In fact, in the frantic rush to get everything done, it is not even seen as an option.

Note that the respect issue here is not only about respect for others but respect for oneself. The person in this example is a dedicated worker with good intentions. Her behavior creates as much, if not more, stress on her than on the others in her teams. She feels bad about the results of her actions but has not learned to change her behavior to change the results.

Working Together

The terms team and teamwork have been so overused that they take away from our ability to truly work together in the spirit of a unified effort. Let's reclaim team and teamwork to blend people's work so that the sum of their contributions is exponential and *not* arithmetic.

> Words are symbols that only point to the objects they describe.
> People working together create an energy that can be felt, experienced in a non-intellectual way.
> Go beyond the words and seek authentic relationships and the experience they create.

A team is a group of people with a common goal. For the most part, projects are performed by teams because they are too big and complex to be done by any individual. While there are projects performed by individuals, they are either personal in nature or parts of larger programs, projects, or processes. Working in teams is a necessity.

Experience with teamwork has shown that there is a continuum of results that ranges from significantly increased productivity and quality to significantly lower productivity and quality, when compared to people working independently. Synergy is the combined effort of two or more things working together being greater than the sum of the individual efforts. Effective teamwork increases synergy. Ineffective teamwork reduces it.

Synergy is enhanced when teamwork brings out:

• peer and self pressure to keep going and focus
• the need to communicate to fully formulate and express ideas
• the need to get consensus and buy-in among the team members
• a broader knowledge pool to enable more possibilities for problem solving.

In a recent yoga course, the teacher kept referring to the need to integrate all the parts of the body so they support and enhance one another to maximize benefits. Don't just pull in your abdomen; lift your chest, adjust your pelvis and legs, and position your head and neck, to get into the posture. Instead, create a holistic balance among the parts. This is the way the members of a team need to work together. The whole is far more than the sum of the parts.

Each member performs his or her work in the context of the team's objectives. They do it in a way that supports and enhances the work of the others and improves the team's ability to achieve its objectives.

Sometimes team members work on tasks that are relatively discrete from one another, sometimes serially, sometimes in parallel. Other times people work together on the same task. The degree to which team members rely on and interact with one another is a major factor in team effectiveness.

The most complex and often the most valuable kind of teamwork is people working together, simultaneously on a single task. This represents the highest degree of reliance and interaction. Here is where the ability to apply effective communications and a Zen attitude is most critical to success. Not to say that these are not important in other kinds of teamwork. They are important as a baseline for any kind of effective collaboration in any relationship.

Example: Concurrent Design

Consider design. Concurrent design evolved in the automotive industry after many years of having designers design cars in a linear process in which specialists in different design areas (engine, interior, body, etc.) each did their part and then someone put the parts of the design together, often requiring changes to individual design elements. The result would eventually get to the manufacturing group and they would make changes yet again to make the design comply with their needs. Often when there was need for a change, different design groups argued about which part of the design should change. Often, as a change was made, its effects rippled through the overall design, causing additional rework and often, conflict.

In concurrent design, the various specialists, including manufacturing and product support people, meet together, establish overall product design, and identify constraints. Then specialized designs are done in the context of the overall design that had considered all the design implications from a big picture point of view. Cooperation and review across specialty disciplines and the people who would have to live with the design made it possible for the designers to find and eliminate design issues early in the process. Early discovery and avoidance of design issues made the design process less costly and more predictable. The time to a workable design is shortened because changes late in the process can be minimized.

The Cost of Teamwork

Of course, there is a price to pay when people work together on a design or any activity.

As their work is more integrated they have to communicate and coordinate more naturally, quickly and interpersonally. Communication, coordination, making decisions, and especially coming to consensus take time, skill, and effort. The cost of the time and effort of all the team members involved in meetings and other communications is high. Keep the cost in synch with the benefits of better solutions that are more easily implemented and overall cost savings.

Teamwork costs can be kept down by enabling people to work in a linear way, independently toward one goal in unison while recognizing where they must work in a more tightly coupled intensive relationship in which the degree of reliance and interaction is high.

This is a delicate balance. Some err to the side of overly minimizing these intensive activities while others err to the side of having everyone work on everything together. Striking the right balance means giving up wishful thinking that a linear approach will work just right the first time and actually cost less and take less time than a concurrent approach. This wishful thinking is often based on the desire to avoid the upfront cost and complexity of having people actively work together in integrated efforts.

In a recent project, one of the participants complained about spending too much time in work sessions. She felt that she could do her work independently. She was right. Her work was to coordinate and to finalize a document being authored by the other members of the team. The authors agreed that the work sessions were essential as a forum to share understandings and work through issues. They wanted the other team member to be present to make her work more effective and to reduce the possibility of error. They also appreciated her input and thought that she would learn from the sessions.

On a personal level, teamwork has another cost (and benefit). It requires interpersonal relationship skills and emotional intelligence. People are *challenged* to see things as others might see them and to question their own positions in the light of critical input. In other words, the cost and benefit of teamwork is doing the inner work that presents itself in relationships.

In our example regarding respect, we have a person who feels bad but doesn't change. If she were a Zen practitioner she would more clearly see her personal responsibility and make her behavior and the feelings that both cause and arise from it fuel for the inner work, she would slow down the process and she would fine tune her scheduling, estimating, and communication skills to better manage expectations.

Our friend Pat, the Zen PM, discovered the power of her practice regarding this issue. In one instance, she was being criticized by her boss for bringing in a project late and over budget. She knew she did her best and that the principle reasons for the project's short fall were outside of her ability to control them. Nevertheless, she felt embarrassed, fearful, frustrated and angry at various times during the session. Thanks to her mindful awareness of her feelings she was able to keep from making excuses and expressing her frustration. Instead she watched her feelings. She gave herself the time to respond rather than react and asked, "How can we avoid this kind of thing the next time?" She engaged her boss in an exploration of the causes of the problem and was able to get him to raise the issues that needed his attention. In the end her frustration melted, her confidence was restored and, while she did not get any explicit acknowledgement, she knew she had made the points she wanted to make.

What Is a Team?

There is the idea that a group is a team just because everyone is working on the same project and therefore they have a common goal.

Webster defines *teamwork* as "Work done by several associates with each doing a part but all subordinating personal prominence to the efficiency of the whole." Cleland and Kerzner in *A Project Management Dictionary of Terms* define teamwork as "Joint action by a group of people, in which individual interests are subordinated to group unity and efficiency. A coordinated effort."

We can all agree that in using these definitions a gaggle of geese is not a team. The geese all share a common objective, they work together. There's a leader. But other than that there is no division of responsibilities, no joint action. That's why we call it a "gaggle" and not a team.

What about horses? We call two or three horses working together a team. Aside from the obvious, how does a team of horses differ from a team of people? With horses there is a human setting the pace, controlling the interactions, training the horses to be obedient and to work together. Horses like working in groups. They are herd animals. They get into a common pace naturally.

Human teams may have a leader but the leadership role is, hopefully, much different than the driver of a team of horses. For one thing, the leader is a member of the same species and is usually not very much smarter than the other team members, if at all. Team members may have significantly greater skills and experience in at least some aspects of the work. Some human teams don't have a single leader at all. Sometimes, leaders treat their team members as if they were horses and some team members actually like being told what to do, as it removes any responsibility from their shoulders.

Further, humans, while being social by nature, are not herd animals and often have little or no training in teamwork. Some say there is a natural proclivity towards social interaction and teamwork. Others say that people, particularly high achievers and excellent performers, tend to prefer individual work or are not so easy to work with. Either way, we come across some people who thrive in the team and others who do far better as individual performers.

So, for our purposes, we will define a team as: a group of people consciously working together to accomplish a common purpose, where the team members subordinate their interests to the interests of the team and the work of individuals is combined to support and enhance team performance.

In the broadest sense, the members of a project team are all the people who are involved in the project: participants, clients, and other interested parties. Any service provider is a member of the team, as are the client and sponsor. Depending on roles, responsibilities, and the way the work is planned, there is a range of reliance and interaction requirements.

Teams—Groups of "I"s

"The work of the individual still remains the spark that moves mankind ahead even more than teamwork."

Igor Sikorsky[55]

Let's get past a major misconception about teams. While the word *team* has no "i," the old saying about there being "no 'I' in team" is simplistic and misleading. Anyone who has ever worked on a team knows that there are many I's. Who are the members? Who does the work? A team is a group of individuals I's. In fact the best teams are peopled by intelligent, high performing individuals with strong egos.

Can you completely eliminate your ego to become a member of an I-less team? If you think you can, you are either delusional or enlightened. Since most of us are neither, it is important to recognize how to *balance* the needs of the individual and the needs of the team, not eliminate the individual egos. With business or project teams, when we talk about "subordinating individual interests" we are not talking in absolutes. It is unrealistic in most project settings to expect a team member to "fall on a grenade" to sacrifice his life for the sake of his teammates. Though in the military we might find such things happening, they are considered above and beyond the call of normal duty and warrant medals. Further, they result from very intensive training and conditioning designed to subordinate individual needs to the needs of the team and mission. A few might aspire to be Bodhisattvas, those selfless fully realized beings who choose to devote their existence to the benefit of all beings. But for the not yet fully realized, we need to be realistic about the way we relate to others.

So what's all this "no 'I' in team" about? It means that for a team to be really effective its members must be willing to subordinate individual preferences to the benefit of the team. We want strong individuals with the skills and experience needed to meet the team's objectives. Paradoxically, it takes a strong individual to give up his/her way when that is best for the team and to stick to his/her way to convince the rest of the team when that is best. Here we have another delicate balance. Go too far in subordinating individual needs and we have an ant colony; not far enough and we have a bunch of prima donnas.

What Is a Healthy Team

Have you worked in a team that really *clicked?* What does *clicked* mean? It is that point when team members experience synchronicity, smooth interaction with just the right amount of communication; members almost read one another's minds and adapt smoothly to their needs, the work gets done "effortlessly." This doesn't imply that there is no friction, no effort. It implies the effective working through of issues collaboratively, rationally, with kindness and joy.

Have you ever worked in a team that never really reached that point?

Informal surveys taken in project management seminars and speaking engagements show that many people have experienced the power of a well functioning healthy team. They report being invigorated, super effective, happy. They have felt a sense of loss when the team separates and they re-form into other teams.

Others report never having a truly powerful and complete team experience. Some have experienced dysfunctional teams in which bickering, politics, internal competition, blaming, and conflict were norms. In these teams, members were sapped of energy and de-motivated.

Between the extremes there are teams with all degrees of health. Some are just OK. The members don't argue much, the work gets done, but something is missing. There is no "magic" no joy.

The common characteristics of healthy teams reported by participants in hundreds of classes were:

Effective and open communications—people could say what they needed to say when they needed to say it; everyone had the information they needed to do their job and know why they were doing their job; there was the "right" amount of documentation

Conscious conflict and conflict resolution, problem solving and decision-making processes were discussed and agreed upon so that people knew how and when to raise, address and escalate issues; conflicts were resolved amicably with the goal of win-win resolutions

Well-defined and communicated objectives—everyone knew and agreed upon what they were doing and why; there was a sense of priorities among objectives; objectives were subject to change during projects; objectives were realistic

A plan—accepted by all participants was used throughout project life as a control point and means for communicating about the project and validating that they were in fact all in agreement

Good meetings—meetings were well planned, people followed

agendas, kept notes and published minutes; meeting schedules were honored so that people generally came on time and the meeting ended when planned

Chemistry—people were kind, compatible and willing to work through their issues and balanced their diverse strengths and weakness among one another without divisive competition, jealousy, grudges and "personality" issues

Good leadership and direction with the minimal degree of hierarchy—leaders articulated goals and values, recognized and acknowledged the importance of every member's contribution, protected the team from unreasonable demands and stress; leaders respected individual members and treated them as equals

Process refinement—team members took opportunities during the project to refine the way people worked together

The right mix of skills and available resources—the right number of people with the right skills and expertise was available to meet the team's objectives.

Continuum: Healthy and Dysfunctional Teams

We know from experience that there is a wide continuum ranging from healthy, super high performance to dismally dysfunctional.

The truly healthy team combines two principle success factors—high accomplishment performance and high quality of life including healthy relations. Teams that only focus on high performance without addressing quality of life are like prison camps in which the inmates are forced to work in a way that leaves them drained. Since in a prison camp inmates have no options and can be replaced by the next batch of prisoners, burn-out is not a problem. Teams that focus primarily on quality of life and underemphasize performance may be very comfortable to work on for some people but don't promote that extra push that leads to high powered performance and accomplishment. Paradoxically, that leads to a poor quality of life for those people who are motivated by high performance and accomplishment. The "magic" needs the power of high performance and accomplishment to work.

The healthy team effectively and efficiently accomplishes its objectives while team members are happy and healthy. This minimizes stress, motivates high performance, and enables using the same people on many projects over time.

"Knowing" When the Team Is Healthy

The analysts among us may say that we need an objective scale with measurement and correlation to empirical field evidence in order to really define a healthy team. While this might be very useful, it is the intuitive, subjective experience that tells us we have a healthy team.

We know without having to go through the analysis. This is the experience beyond intellect that is an essential element of Zen.

We know from experience that there are many possibilities. Even those without the experience of working in a high performance/high quality of life team have a sense of the way these teams might work and feel from hearing about them from others or watching action movies and reality shows. We can certainly tell when we are suffering with a dysfunctional team without counting the number of unnecessary arguments or measuring our own brainwaves and the brainwaves of some of our more difficult team mates. Here is another opportunity to come in touch with authentic experience. What does it feel like to work well with others?

Essential Ingredients

What are the *essential* ingredients of a healthy team? We can summarize the nine elements identified above into:

Communication
Relationship
Vision
Resource

One ingredient to effective teamwork is the ability to define and evaluate the team's interpersonal process, the combination of relationship and communication. If the team members have a common sense of what a healthy team is like and can assess the way they are performing and behaving against a common benchmark, they have the principle ingredient of team health—the process consciousness discussed in the previous chapter. Without it, teamwork is like baking bread without flour.

Some have worked on healthy teams that had no formal process assessment and no process consciousness. But when that experience is analyzed you will find that usually there was an agreed upon paradigm (which may have been unstated) and an ability to communicate, particularly when things were not going well, in order to fine tune the way people worked together.

Healthy teams may be engineered. They may happen by luck. They may happen because a group has a common sense of what healthy teams are like and their environment supports or at least doesn't inhibit team health. Healthy teams may then operate without much formal discussion and assessment. Engineering health means consciously addressing the team process.

We should teach children how to work in healthy teams so that by the time they get into the world of commercial projects they will be ready to simply expect health as a standard way of operating and they will have the skills required to promote and maintain health.

Storming to address and resolve conflict is as critical a part of team health as any of the other aspects of team building[56]. The team optimizes its performance by adjusting the things about team members' behaviors that are getting in the way of effective cooperation. The adjusting is optimally a natural outcome of mature individuals with good social skills and a desire to work together communicating about their feelings and expectations.

> **The more the individuals naturally adjust to perfect their process, the more it seems as if there is no process consciousness. It is all just happening in the normal flow of team activity.**

Process Consciousness

We are not always so fortunate as to be on teams with all mature, competent and well socialized individuals. Even the best of us forget ourselves every so often and get lost in our thoughts and emotions. We may become ego-centric and get angry or disappointed when things don't go the way we want them to. Perhaps we may fail to speak up when annoyed or abused and then harbor feelings of resentment which lead to anger. We may get so caught up in our own work that we begin to optimize it at the expense of others, as in our earlier example.

Here is an opportunity for inner work.

With mindfulness and process consciousness, these moments of forgetting can be minimized. The individual can mindfully remember to be present and to work in a way that fully supports the needs of others as well as one's own needs. The team as a whole can do the same thing by consciously addressing process issues and resolving them through open dialogue and effective problem solving; combining communication and relationship.

> There is no blame for forgetting and getting lost in the mind.
> It occurs. Recognize it. Return to presence. Begin again.
> Of these, recognizing is the most significant.
> The moment you realize that you are lost in your thoughts and emotions and have become reactive is a moment of enlightenment.

Engineering Health

The less the members of a team are familiar with working together and the greater the mix of people with different degrees of experience and training in teamwork, the more it is necessary to have a more formal team process to highlight and promote team health.

Formal process teaches the members to operate effectively on the team; it provides a common language and includes techniques such as decision-making processes, meeting checklists and protocols for avoiding and addressing issues that may arise. As the team becomes more experienced, the process integrates into normal behavior and becomes *almost* unconscious. It is like watching a champion skier who has mastered his sport and performs so that it seems effortless. Of course if the process becomes unconscious, the inner work is interrupted. That *almost* is a very important thing. Pay just enough attention to process to provide the lubricant for fluid and effective teamwork. Let that attention become an unobtrusive awareness.

> **Moment to moment mindfulness coupled with process consciousness provides an edge to optimize performance.**

An effective team can be engineered. But the time and effort to engineer a healthy, high performing team varies widely depending on a number of factors. The health of the team's environment, the "chemistry" among the members, the degree to which they "look at their process" and whether they are willing to change their behavior to accommodate the team's needs all effect the effort to engineer a healthy team. The degree to which members are conscious of themselves, their behavior and the way it impacts others is a critical factor. The degree to which members are kind, ethical, and compassionate is another.

It is one thing to believe in the ability to engineer healthy teams, but it is not particularly effective to rely on belief. In the Zen way we test the belief. How can we cultivate health and maintain it?

A healthy team rests on the concrete foundation of the right number of competent people who clearly understand their roles and responsibilities, have an effective communications plan, and have commonly understood and measurable goals and objectives. Project success is founded on this.

But true health goes beyond the ability to set a concrete foundation and build a process. True health requires individuals who are able, at least sometimes, to be self reflective enough to enter into healthy relationships, who are motivated and who can see the big picture as well as their place in it. True health requires presence, a systems perspective and the ability to "step outside of oneself" to give and accept criticism without defensiveness.

Notice that there is no "must" here. No absolute statement. We all know it is possible to work in less than ideal circumstances. Team health is another continuum; an opportunity to find optimum balance.

> Perfection includes the imperfections that are naturally occurring in the real world and the ability to work with them to reach new degrees of perfection.
> Can we reach perfection?
> "Let's see" is the only right answer.

The engineering of a healthy team is a continuous improvement process.

Chemistry and Compatibility

Chemistry among team members refers, in part, to the degree to which they share common values and styles. If they do not, more effort is needed to work together.

"Team chemistry is one of the most complicated keys to the success of organizations. Effective teams are more than just a collection of talented members. To be effective, a team has to be able to combine the efforts and abilities of members in the right way. Just as no two people are identical, no two teams are identical. Consequently, what works well for one team may not work well for others. However, research has identified several factors that usually produce good team chemistry:

- Diversity
- Role taking
- Constructive norms
- Leadership
- Cohesiveness
- "Common vision"[57]

Differences, particularly differences in values, can get in the way of working together smoothly. For example, if some members of a team believe that it is best to withhold criticism to avoid conflict and others believe that constructive criticism in public view is beneficial, then the team will experience conflict. The team can get hung up on this issue, letting it poison relationships and inhibit quality performance and continuous improvement. Alternatively the team can resolve the issue, using differences as a catalyst and as strength.

In one case, a team member objected when his work was criticized in a review process and became so angry at other team members that he refused to work with them again. To this team member, the criticism was too harsh and unwarranted. To the other members of the team the criticism was strictly about the content of the work as opposed to the individual. The criticized team member would not discuss the issue. "This is the way I see it and there is no sense in discussing it any further," he declared at one point.

In the end, this team was healthy enough to eliminate the team member. In other situations, the team member may be retained but managed by the others in a way that compensates for his blind spot. But there are many examples in which people with conflicting beliefs and styles must continue to work together without really addressing their relationship issues. They tacitly agree to work together inefficiently and often unpleasantly.

In another example, a team member found that he had to resign from a team because he refused to work in a team that did <u>not</u> allow for critical analysis of performance. He felt that it was better to opt out than to continue to live with mediocre results and dysfunction.

The choice to speak up, act, accommodate, or opt out is a personal choice drive by a number of factors. From the Zen perspective, recognition that it is a personal choice is a step towards accepting the reality and working with it.

Values

A value is a principle or quality that has high worth because it is of great use or service. Values are mental models and mental models are subjected to scrutiny because they drive behavior. Unstated and unconscious values get in the way.

In project teams, values include the importance of open and sensitive criticism and of adjustments in behavior based on critical feedback. Truthfulness, honesty, kindness, peer vs. hierarchical relationships, balance between project work, and other activities including personal life, and a positive work ethic are other values. Differences regarding values often result in conflicts in day to day relationships. As a rule of thumb, if there are frequent conflicts about concrete issues or a general sense of dissatisfaction with team relationships, explore differences in values as a possible cause.

Perhaps the most critical aspects of *chemistry* are the degree to which people have a common value about working through their differences and the degree to which they respect one another as individuals.

Underlying the Zen way is an overriding value of compassion. When we recognize that we are all in the same boat we can more easily accept others' behaviors. Accepting other peoples' behaviors doesn't mean liking them or supporting them or even allowing them to continue. It simply means seeing them for what they are long enough to respond rather than react. Compassion, in this context, is the ability to *feel* for the other person because you understand their situation. You understand it not because you have some analytical insight into their personal issues, but because you can recognize the common underlying condition you share. You can empathize.

There is fairly general agreement that kindness, generosity, not doing harm or killing, not stealing, seeking to improve, and telling the truth are positive values. There is some controversy about other values like taking intoxicants; killing, lying and stealing for 'good' cause; having sex out of wedlock or at all; taking or giving bribes; among many others. There is further controversy about whether positive values should be applied only within one's own group. For example, "Don't kill or steal from people who are of your religion, tribe, country, company or race, but it is okay to kill or steal from others."

As with all complex issues, don't overdo it. Project teams are focused on getting work done. Discussions about values should be limited to the degree that they add value. But, don't avoid these discussions when they are needed. Values are difficult to address and there is a common avoidance method that paints them as being "too philosophical" and impractical. Confront values issues and resolve them, ideally, when the team is forming and storming.

Styles

Working with diverse styles is easier than working with differences in values. With a bit of understanding about the nature of the differences and some ability to control emotional reactions and respond in a way that promotes teamwork, people learn to accept the differences, see the strength in blending different styles on a team, and become less reactive to behaviors that are abrasive to their style.

There are a number of character styles models, including Meyers-Briggs, DISC, and the Boltons' Social and Thinking Styles model. These enable members of a team to learn one another's styles as well as their own and to apply the learning to create healthier team relationships. In effect these models help people recognize that most of other peoples' bothersome behaviors are the result of their natural tendencies or styles and that the behaviors are not personally directed at them.

The clash between these styles and the often unconscious expectation that "everyone should behave the way I want them to" underlies much of the conflict in teams. Simply recognizing that it is possible to flex one's style and expectations about other peoples' behavior leads to healthier relationships. Add to that the practice of observing one's reactions before they become behaviors and moderating them to the needs of the situation, and there is a great possibility of improved effectiveness in any relationship.

Example: Cutting through Style Differences

Our friend Pat the Zen PM provides an example of how awareness and communication can help to cut through style differences. She had two people working together on a project, one very analytical and the other more intuitive, right-brain oriented. These two were in constant conflict as the analytical person rejected the intuitive findings of the other team member and the right-brain-er minimized the importance of analysis and constantly focused on the big picture and "feelings." The two argued about why and when to take action, even when they were more or less in agreement about what action to take.

Pat watched her own impatience. She put herself in each of their shoes and felt their frustration. She thought that if these two spent some time addressing their differences they might find that the combination of their approaches enhanced team performance and their individual effectiveness, particularly if they got to be a bit more patient and more willing to shift their style. She set out to influence them. Setting up a work session among the three of them, she facilitated a discussion about the strengths and weaknesses of each style. By the end of the session, there was a meeting of the minds, an understanding that led to a far easier and more effective working relationship.

Diversity

Diversity goes beyond personal styles. It includes cultural differences. There are national and ethnic as well as organizational cultures.

People raised and habituated in different cultures have different values and behaviors. People from some cultures tend to be more or less oriented to getting things done on time. Others may have difficulty saying no or may say it differently than others. Handling conflict and criticism vary across cultures. There are differences in the amount of physical distance that is comfortable between people having a conversation as well as whether physical contact is appropriate. The meanings of words and symbols as well as body language differ.

These differences are sources of potential conflict in teams. It is wise to address them openly, along with differences in values and personal styles as the team is forming. A healthy team is one in which there is room for diversity *and* in which the members are willing to adapt to the needs of their team by giving up those culturally conditioned behaviors that are there only because they are conditioned. The ability to tell the difference between those behaviors that may be subject to change and those that are tied to religious and other beliefs that people consciously choose to adhere to is a challenge.

For example, a culturally based tendency to come late to meetings can and could be changed as it is disruptive and wastes time and effort and is not tied to any known religious belief or strongly held cultural value. A cultural or religious need for no touching between men and women, particular styles of dress, and other observances should be understood and honored.

In the end, behaviors that work against the team meeting its objectives should be changed. To the degree that the team can adapt to the diverse needs of its members without jeopardizing its mission, it should. Finding the right balance requires consciously discussing the issues, planning to address them and working through conflicts and problems as they arise during the project. If the upfront discussion and planning were done well, there will be fewer conflicts and problems and the ones that arise will be easier to address.

Learning from Relationships

Relationships of any kind are challenging. Among the greatest benefits from working on teams is the opportunity to learn to work with people who are different, particularly those who "push our buttons" to trigger emotional reactions. If you take on the exercise: Exploring the Cause of Emotions, introduced earlier in this chapter, you will soon see the connections between the button and the reaction.

The team is a place where we are often confronted with people who we may not choose to otherwise spend time with. Even if when we do choose the people to spend time with, we soon find that they are different from us and different from how we expected them to be. So, if we are able, we adapt to the differences and modify behavior to promote synergy.

We can use the opportunity in the quest for self-actualization. We do this by seeing our emotional or habitual reactions and working to understand where they come from in ourselves so we can decide how best to behave in the moment and free ourselves from being reactive.

To blame another for one's reactions is common but unwise. If someone pushes your button, you have the power to disconnect your reaction from the button. External behavior is a stimulus. Reactive behavior in response to the stimulus can be worked with to increasingly enable conscious choice. There is a switch between the button and the response. One way, the switch triggers reactive behavior. The other way, there are a number of alternative behaviors to choose from.

Working towards self-actualization is above and beyond the reasonable expectations of many people. It is your choice to continue being reactive or to take responsibility for your behavior and throw the switch.

"If someone hits me, I hit them back." "If someone insults me it is their fault that I explode angrily or get back at them." These are commonly held beliefs that the wise go beyond, in taking responsibility for their behavior.

"Turn the other cheek" if you can, but whatever you do, do it consciously with the bigger picture in mind. In projects the bigger picture is the ability to get the job done efficiently and effectively. In life it is the ability to learn from everything, as Maslow says, "to be what you can be."

Hierarchy

> "A boss creates fear, a leader confidence.
> A boss fixes blame, a leader corrects mistakes.
> A boss knows all, a leader asks questions.
> A boss makes work drudgery, a leader makes it interesting.
> A boss is interested in himself or herself, a leader is interested in the group."
>
> Russell H. Ewing[58]

Given the challenges of working with people who have different values, levels of understanding and capacity, and different styles and cultural tendencies, working in teams is pretty complex. To make it even more complex we throw in hierarchies with their implications concerning power, authority, and fear.

Hierarchies are created whenever one person or group has or is perceived to have more power or higher value than others. The project manager who has the authority to make work assignments, set schedules, and evaluate performance is "above" the team members in a hierarchy. The PM is usually below the sponsor and client in a hierarchy of power and influence and possibly above them in a hierarchy of knowledge and capability in the project. The more complex the project and its environment, the more complex are the hierarchical relationships.

Position in a hierarchy coupled with cultural, style, and value differences create a dynamic that can be both a barrier to and a means to promote effective performance.

Stephen Covey says, "The more a manager controls, the more he/she evokes behaviors that necessitate greater control or managing."[59] He is using the term "control" to mean telling people what to do.

When a team member says "Yes sir" and goes off without questioning to perform some task they think is stupid or impossible, it is an example of how hierarchy gets in the way of effective behavior. Covey goes on to say that authoritarian behavior tends to reduce initiative. It trains people to wait to be told what to do and to feel separated from the work. They might be thanked for their "cooperation and support" but the fame or blame goes to the manager.

If the team member questions authority he may learn the reason for the task and, maybe, realize that it is neither stupid nor impossible. He may stimulate a reevaluation of the task by the power(s) that be, and they may revise their direction. He may also reinforce his belief that the task is in fact stupid or impossible and learn more about the nature of his leadership and management.

On the other hand, there are situations where following orders without question is the thing to do.

> Once again we have paradox and continuum— **not this or that but the right degrees of this and that to suit the situation.**

As a PM and team member it is critical that you determine when and how to question authority. Watch your reactions. Are you reacting to not being the one in control? Are you overusing your authority or under using it? Exercising too much control and power underutilizes the skill and expertise of the team. It may de-motivate by <u>not</u> getting the buy-in that can be obtained only with collaborative decision-making across the hierarchy. Is there fear underlying the reactions? Is the fear well founded, and how can it best be handled intrapersonally and interpersonally?

A primary cause of fear in hierarchies is insecurity. "If I displease the boss I will be fired, not get my next raise or yelled at." Managing fear is tricky. If one is too fearless and ignores the signal that fear represents, one can get fired or relegated to the "difficult person" category and face marginal career advancement, if any. If one is driven by fear, then personal decisions become irrational. There is insufficient push-back against unrealistic demands. There is a sense of being abused and taken advantage of. This last result leads to animosity and depression.

As the one higher up in the hierarchy, do whatever is possible to create a safe environment in which authority is minimally used and in which there are clear and reasonable criteria for performance evaluation; evaluation of you as a leader/manager and of others in their positions.

As the one lower down, look to your own conditioning, your psychological issues and the reality of your physical situation and do your best to acknowledge and accept your fear but not be driven by it.

Feel the fear, let it fill your mind and body, and then step back from it to see what the cause is and what can best be done about it. Simple; not so easy, but doable. This capacity to be a calm observer of one's own strong feelings, without being reactive is cultivated using the mindfulness techniques to be formally presented in the next chapter.

Alternatives to Hierarchical Organization

As one who is in a position to establish the hierarchy in a project, consider teams of peers and leaderless teams as alternatives to traditional hierarchical organizations. These models do not completely eliminate authority. They recognize that the authority to make certain decisions, including the approval of other peoples' decisions and evaluation of their work is a very useful, if not necessary, part of performing projects. These models recognize that while a person may have authority in one area it does not imply that the person is better, smarter, stronger or higher-up than anyone else. Authority is a part of a role definition. It is a means to the end for effective performance.

The 360˚ review approach discussed in chapter 7, on quality and people, further supports the idea that while authority is a fact of life, accountability for one's behaviors to everyone one works with is necessary to promote team health.

Informal Teams

Whether it is an alternative to or something that operates in parallel with formal team structures, there are informal teams that are networks of people who rely on one another outside of normal channels and hierarchies. Their reliance is based on cultivated relationships. Daniel Goleman, in explaining the difference between star performers and others quotes Robert Kelley and Janet Caplan's article, "How Bell Labs Creates Star Performers":

A middle performer at Bell Labs talked about being stumped by a technical problem. He painstakingly called various technical Gurus and then waited, wasting valuable time while calls went unreturned and e-mails unanswered. Star performers, however, rarely face such situations because they do the work of building reliable networks before they actually need them. When they call someone for advice, stars almost always get an answer fast.[60]

The informal network operates without hierarchies and is based on interpersonal relationships that are strong enough to motivate busy people to take the time and effort to help someone out even though it is not on their formal task and responsibility list. It is this willingness to help that differentiates the merely adequate from the excellent.

Yet we find that many projects are organized and planned to make such informal activity difficult or impossible. Tight deadlines and over-control motivate people to protect their time. Their deadlines are so tight that the 'space' to operate informally is squeezed out and replaced by hierarchical and bureaucratic processes.

Again, we must find the right balance, blending the right amounts of informal, nonhierarchical activity with the right degree of control and cost and time consciousness.

Who Is in and Who Is Out?

Yet another aspect of the team dynamic is the sense of belonging vs. being an outsider.

Certainly limiting the number of people copied on e-mails and involved in work sessions and meetings are good things, but are there any negatives?

> Everything has a shadow side.
> Chocolate cake is a good thing but even to a cake-eating chocolate lover, there is a negative side—weight gain and other health issues for example.

In the case of excluding people from communications, the positives are efficiency and security. Limiting the number of people involved in decision-making reduces complexity and the amount of time and effort involved. Those who are excluded do not know about the subject and therefore do not have the ability to breach security.

The negative effects of exclusion may or may *not* outweigh the positives. Inclusion and exclusion are management decisions and like all management decisions they require weighing the long and short term benefits against the liabilities and risks.

The liabilities and risks of excluding people from communications in the short term include loss of their input and greater difficulty in getting their buy-in regarding the outcome or decision. On the softer side and longer term there are the potentials for loss of trust and loss of team cohesion.

Consider the team member who, unknown to him, is excluded from a decision-making process that affects his role on the project and is on a subject that he thinks is one he is expert in. This can lead to bad feelings and, in turn, to a lack of buy-in to the decision, even if it is a good one. There may be the sense of being considered not good-enough by one's boss or peers, or of feeling that "The others are fools for not bringing me in on this decision. Do I really want to work with fools? Do I want to work with people who do not value my input?"

Consider the same situation in which the left-out member is informed in advance that he is being or may be left out of decisions and why. Would reactions be the same? Here we come back to expectations and the management of them to satisfy stakeholders, including project performers. If the working agreements created at the onset of a project explicitly address this aspect of involvement, expectations will be managed and the likelihood of negative reactions will be low.

The short term issues of loss of input and greater difficulty in getting buy-in are pretty concrete. The fewer people in a decision-making group, the less input; the more people, the greater the cost and effort. Consciously decide why and whom to include to ensure that the benefits will out weigh the negatives.

The creative manager can address getting buy-in through editing and review, effective communications, and change management in the implementation of the decision. Loss of the value of the excluded input is a calculated risk that can be moderated by the right level of invited critical feedback.

Trust and Team Cohesion

Team cohesion refers to the degree to which the team has *clicked,* the degree to which members recognize their mutual needs and act upon them in their relationships. Trust is a critical determinant of team cohesion and health. It is a foundation for relationship. The impact of distrust is described by Covey in terms of the symptoms of "backbiting, in-fighting, victimization, defensiveness, information hoarding, and defensive, protective communication."[61]

> Trust is not intellectual. What is your experience of the sensation of trusting or of not trusting? This in itself is a Zen exercise that takes you out of your intellect.
>
> Are you awake? When was the last time you were aware of your breath, your thoughts?

Trust is lost in many ways—lack of truthfulness, evidence of unethical behavior, misunderstood or divergent motivation, a sense of feeling excluded, poor communication, paranoia, and projection. For example, in the context of team membership or involvement, when an unannounced exclusion is realized, the excluded parties may have a sense of there being an entire realm of which they are unaware. Not saying is not so far from lying in many people's minds. Depending on personality and position, this may cause internal conflicts, unnecessary assumptions and a sense that something is going on around them that is being purposely kept from them. They may begin to question and fantasize the reasons for exclusion. "They don't trust me." "They don't value my input." "They want to manipulate me." Paranoia begins to reign.

Paranoia coupled with the sense that one is not valued or trusted creates a gap among team members. Perhaps the included group feels distrusted by those in the excluded group, increasing or creating the gap. A hierarchy is perceived (ins are better than outs), and hierarchies can drive wedges between people in teams.

Recap

People and their relationships are the bedrock foundation of projects—no people, no work; no work, no results. Teams are people working together. Healthy teams are teams that overcome individual differences to 'click' into a synergistic process that exponentially enhances the power of the individual members.

Conscious attention to the way the work is done and, particularly, to the way people relate to one another is the key to healthy teams. Conscious attention is just another application of mindfulness. As long as we are mindful of our surroundings, our inner selves, and the effect we have on those around us, we can do the self adjusting that is needed to blend with the other members of the team. The result is a single optimally performing unit, one made up of strong individuals who make a concerted effort to subordinate their needs to the needs of the team.

Managing expectations is a key to healthy teams. Set expectations at the start of a project or at any critical point at which new people are joining the team or there are recognized problems. The planning and project kick-off process should address the team's values and objectives, how communication will take place, how decisions will be made, who has what roles and responsibilities, how much and what kind of 'pushback' is expected, how and on what criteria performance will be evaluated, how issues will be raised, addressed, and escalated, how interpersonal differences will be addressed, how authority will be exercised, and why these "soft" issues are critical to success.

Healthy teams may just happen, but they are far more likely to happen if they are engineered. In any case, mindfulness, compassion, kindness, and a sense of openness to the needs of others are the most critical elements to promote both the inner and outer work.

Chapter 11

Managing From Your Center

Overview

Responsive, fluid, effective, efficient, realistic, focused, mindful, aware, ethical, compassionate, sensitive, skillful, and knowledgeable—these are attributes of a master project manager. It is the individual's responsibility to cultivate these qualities in order to continuously improve personally and professionally. Each attribute is one flower, beautiful and important on its own. Together they are an arrangement that creates beauty that is above and beyond the beauty of each.

Most of the other chapters in this book have addressed the outer work and the way it is used in the inner wok. This chapter is focused directly on the inner work. It recaps some of the core Zen principles. It explores the experience of being *centered,* or being in touch with one's *psycho/spiritual core.* Insight meditation is presented as the principle method for cultivating greater ability to rise above reactive behavior by seeing things objectively. This method is the means for getting and staying centered and for cutting through the barriers to self-actualization.

Escape from Waterfall Mind

How often are we caught up in the whirlwind of activities that are our thoughts, our projects, our work, and our relationships? When we are caught up, the ability to perform and manage is reduced. We make errors both in the content of our work and the way we relate with others. The result is unnecessary rework, conflict, and suffering.

When caught up, we do not see the big picture. It is as if we are in a waterfall. The speed of current events, fixation on short-range objectives, anxiety, and emotions all combine to cloud broader vision. The water is flowing so fast and furiously that we can see only what is right in front of us. We become reactive.

If you have never experienced "waterfall mind," you may have no need to read further. On the other hand, you may be so used to waterfall mind that you don't realize there is an alternative.

However, the fact that you have gotten this far indicates awareness of the need to explore this dimension of mind. When in the midst of complex relationships, stress, pressure to meet tight (if not impossible) deadlines within rigid budgets, there is a *performance edge* that comes from being centered.

Being centered is having the sense of no longer being in the waterfall. One may be slightly *behind* the waterfall. The water is still falling but it slows down in your perception.

The internal chatter—intrusive thoughts—can be seen and slowed. When we do this, there is the sense of being able to see all around, to see where one is going; where one has been. All around, the whirlwind of activities continues. We may have the ability to change it or not. Either way we are in it and behind it simultaneously, active, perceptive, responsive, and in touch with the calm clear space that we can refer to as our center.

To Respond, Not React

It is best to respond, not react. Being centered, there is presence of mind to plan, assess risk, and resolve problems without leaving unnecessary side-effects; in short to be more effective.

Reactivity is acting out of our emotions. Emotions are defined in dictionaries as strong feelings and the agitation or disturbance caused by them. An emotion is a complex of psychological and physical feelings that are strong enough to create a distinct pressure to react. There are many emotions, including anger, joyfulness, sadness, fear, love, and shame. Each is complex. For example, fear may manifest as terror, anxiety, or concern; anger as fury, resentment or annoyance; joyfulness as pleasure, thrill, contentment, or ecstasy.

Being driven by emotions implies being lost to rational thought. There is action without assessing the consequences. Controlling the response to emotions, not burying or denying them, is a key to effective behavior. Being able to moderate one's behavior is the cornerstone of emotional intelligence and effective relationships. Effective relationships are the cornerstone of effective performance in organizations and projects. Of course, managing one's emotions is hard work.

Daniel Goleman says there are two kinds of emotional reactions. One is very quick, the other more deliberate, taking time for emotional pressure to build as one ruminates over how they've been cheated or poorly treated, for example.

In the quick reaction, the time between a stimulus and emotional response is "virtually instantaneous … reckoned in thousandths of a second."[62] The rational mind takes a moment or two longer to register and respond. As a result there is a tendency to reactively behave to handle the emotion. While this quick emotional responsiveness is quite important as an adaptive mechanism to survive in the wild, it is less effective in the context of interpersonal relationships at work.

The slower form of emotion arises out of a thinking process that begins with a thought usually triggered by some event or volitionally brought to mind to create the emotion. What follows is a sequence of thoughts that build up into an emotion.

When a thought arises into consciousness it begins to build a momentum. We give it energy and attention by holding on to it and by reinforcing it with other thoughts, like "Yeah, that guy really did me wrong. I should have said … Of course I'm angry, look what he did. I have a right to be angry!"

Goleman states that "… the rational mind does not decide what emotions we 'should' have. Instead, our feelings typically come to us as a fait accompli. What the rational mind can ordinarily control is the course of those reactions."[63]

Of course, learning to control the emotions is a challenge. Being centered is having the presence of mind that permits responsive behavior. Being centered supports presence of mind, increasing its duration and the frequency of its occurrence.

To some this may sound like sitting back and thinking for a while before acting. While that may be part of it, responsive as opposed to reactive behavior is also operating from moment to moment, instantaneously. When some problem comes up, maybe there is an hour or a day to respond. But when an event occurs in a phone conversation or a meeting, the response must be in real time. Consider the expert athlete or martial artist, acting spontaneously in perfect alignment with the needs of the moment.

Emotional reaction or reliance on habitual responses often makes things worse. The ability to creatively respond rather then react separates the merely adequate from the good and great. In the wisdom teachings it is said that the person who is truly centered can act and speak spontaneously with complete confidence. Discursive thought is replaced by direct action.

Example: Knowing When to Resist and When to Insist

Reactive behavior is more likely to cause problems than solve them. Consider the following example of a small project that was suspended just before its outcome—a new version of an existing product—was to be released for general use.

The current version of the product was adequate, but required a highly skilled facilitator/operator to fill in the blanks and overcome its weaknesses. The project to create the new version was running late.

Then a new but related project arose. A customized version of the product was to be delivered to a client in a tight time frame. As the new project was being initiated, the question of whether to use the new or old product as the 'base' for the client was explored.

On one hand, the new version was ready to be reviewed and tested, but the client's time schedule did not allow for the testing, editing, and revision required for completing it. On the other hand, the person scheduled to work with the client had the skill and the support to either pull off the use of the old version with little risk, or to work with an imperfect and unknown version and still succeed in delivering an acceptable custom product to the client.

The product manager and quality manager recommended using the old version. The manager of the client project, who was also a key player in the revision project, argued that the unedited version was better than the old one, and insisted on using it. The account executive agreed, without looking at the actual content. They talked the sponsor into the idea that by using the new version and having the client edit it during the customization process, the overall cost of development would be less because the editing would be paid for by the client.

On its own, an issue like this one, even though there may be no one right answer, can be rationally decided. But in this case, emotions ran high, as the issue at hand was intertwined with recriminations about being late in the first place, the way testing and review were sped through in an attempt to save money, and other process and personality issues among the sponsor, product developers, subject matter experts, and marketing.

Some members of the team realized that an emotional argument was counterproductive; they voiced their objection and the reasons for it, and deferred to the others. They did *not* bury their feelings, particularly anger. Instead, they acknowledged them, experienced them, and moved on. Though they believed that the decision was being made without sufficient input from them, they assessed the situation objectively and realized that given the time to make the decision, the risks, and the emotional charge, further resistance would be unproductive. Note that if they had strongly believed that the decision was unworkable as opposed to unwise, they would have been obligated to resist more strongly.

In the end, when the new 'base' product finally got reviewed by the quality team, they found that it was in need of considerable rework before it could be released for general use. The client engagement and the custom changes made for it had been done in a way that momentarily satisfied the client (who had far lower quality standards than the product quality team) but violated several quality control criteria and disregarded earlier design decisions. The additional rework would more than wipe out the gains from the client customization. The project would be further delayed.

When the sponsor reacted angrily to the additional costs and delay, the manager of the client project refused to take responsibility for any part she played in the problem. Fingers were pointed at the product manager and quality team who were accused of being too perfectionist.

Though angry and disappointed with the result, the product manager and quality manager were able to dispassionately address the issues candidly and in a way that defused emotional reactions by bringing a fact-based analysis into the situation.

Rather than getting into blaming and subjective argument, they briefly described the current situation and the way it was reached, labeled assumptions as assumptions and risks as risks, listed defects and their causes, and left the decision to the team. When the team, including the sponsor, became aware of the degree of the quality shortfall, the decision-making was easy. The new version was completed and rolled out.

The real ending is a sad one, though. The group never collectively analyzed its performance and process and the learning was left to chance.

Note how all of the elements of project management are interacting in the story: expectations, process awareness, interpersonal relations and teamwork, hierarchies, emotional intelligence, communication, mindfulness, and awareness.

> At first it seems as if being centered leads to being distanced from the present moment.
> But it is not that. It is to simultaneously see what is happening and what is needed, calmly and clearly, while being completely immersed in the situation.

Working from Your Center

What, then, is working from one's center? It is the ability to come in contact with the calm, peaceful place inside; seeing things objectively; clearly. One's center is a state of mind, not a place. Being centered is characterized by *presence,* along with a sense of being calm, stable, open, fluid, objective, and actively engaged.

"We first thought of presence as being fully conscious and aware in the present moment. Then we began to appreciate presence as deep listening, of being open beyond one's preconceptions and historical ways of making sense… Ultimately, we came to see all these aspects of presence as leading to a state of "letting come," of consciously participating in a larger field for change. When this happens, the field shifts, and the forces shaping a situation can shift from recreating the past to manifesting or realizing an emerging future."[64]

> "We convince by our presence.".
> Walt Whitman

The awareness of being centered has been recognized for thousands of years in wisdom traditions around the world from Christianity to Taoism, Buddhism, and Islam's mystical Sufism. "Taoist theory speaks of the transformation of vital energy, *qing,* (pronounced "ching"), into subtle life force, *qi* (pronounced "chee") and into spiritual energy, *shin.* This process involves an essential quieting of the mind that Buddhists call "cessation," where the normal flow of thoughts ceases and the normal boundaries between self and world dissolve… Each religion describes the shift a little differently, but all recognize it as being central to personal cultivation or maturation."[65]

In Buddhism, the state of "completion" is described as being simultaneously without limits, never created, never ending, empty, and having cognitive potential or the ability to be aware. When we are in touch with this, we are fully present and experiencing our true nature.

Flow

Often, in sports or other physical activity, we experience the sense of being in *flow*. The same sense is felt by artists, writers, designers, and many others when they are most productive. They are completely at one with the moment to moment flow of efforts and events. They are concentrated, active, yet have a broad perspective.

In his book, *Good Business,*[66] Mihaly Csikszentmihalyi uses the term "flow" for the state of consciousness experienced by people when they are deeply engaged, genuinely enjoying the moment, and performing optimally. Based on interviews with tens of thousands of individuals around the world, the flow experience was found to be elicited by eight conditions which combined in various ways to absorb the individual in the performance of an activity. The conditions are as applicable to rock climbing as they are to working on projects.

In the following section are these eight conditions with my comments and their relationship to project management and one another. Among these conditions are some that are causative and others that are results of the causative conditions and of flow itself. Flow reinforces flow.

Clear goals, immediate feedback, balance between opportunity and capacity and the integration of control into the process naturally result in concentration, focus on the present, distortion of time and loss of ego follow. But flow can be engineered. Concentration becomes the key element. As one chooses to concentrate on the task at hand, no matter what it is, the causative conditions are created volitionally and they then have the effect of reinforcing concentration and one another to elicit the focus on the present, on timelessness and egoless-ness. Let's explore each of the conditions in some more depth.

Eight Conditions of Flow

Clear Goals. A focus on the immediate task at hand, moment by moment enables flow. The project manager who is too concerned with hitting the deadline date is not sufficiently attentive to the needs for quality results and of support and operational stakeholders. Here there is a paradox: short term moment to moment focus on tasks while needing to also keep the ultimate goal in mind.

The project manager and team must be focused on the short range plan and the next tasks to be accomplished. Of course, among those short range tasks is the continuous evaluation of progress against the plan and whether the plan should be changed. Taking the step back to review and evaluate is part of the process. The most effective view combines short term goals in the context of the big picture.

Feedback is immediate. Knowing that what one does matters enhances the sense of total involvement. People stay absorbed when they get timely, "real time" feedback about how they are doing. In project work formal feedback is provided by status reports, quality reviews and tests, and comments from peers and team leaders. Feedback to the performers is as important as feedback to the client and sponsor. Informal feedback happens moment to moment as people interact in small work groups and as they see and evaluate their own results in the context of values and objectives.

There is *balance between opportunity and capacity.* The work itself and the performer's skills must be in balance. Every activity is an opportunity to experience flow. People will recognize their capacity and match it to the needs of the opportunity. They will excel, learn or withdraw as the situation's needs dictate.

In projects, when the work is beyond the capacity of the team, stress and disappointment will make flow impossible to sustain. When the capacity is beyond the opportunity and is "too easy", the challenge is to apply full concentration and perfect performance to overcome the tendency to become bored with the work at hand. In other words, make the trivial and boring a focus of attention and transform it into a meditation.

Work like the Zen monk who is so absorbed in washing the dishes, while making sure each dish comes out shining clean and none are broken, that he becomes enlightened. He made the trivial task a meditation on the perfection of the work and the simultaneous perfection of attention and mindfulness.

Concentration deepens. Concentration is holding the mind steady on an object. It is both a cause and effect of flow. Concentration brings about a calm state in which "things just happen." The need to think about and control action is replaced by the natural flow of events.

Concentration can be cultivated. When engaged in an activity that has clear goals, feeds back information and challenges one's ability, there is a natural tendency to become concentrated – involved and absorbed. Even unimportant things like video games or not very useful things like creating a melodrama in one's mind can hold one's attention.

By cultivating concentration the natural tendency for it to arise is reinforced. It happens more frequently, even when external conditions are not eliciting it. Like the Zen monk washing the dishes, you can concentrate and be in flow.

Simply choosing an object and bringing the mind back to it when you become distracted builds concentration. Concentration elicits high performance, calm quiet stillness of the mind and joy.

The present is what matters. With concentration, clear short term goals and immediate feedback, the present comes into focus. "Be here now." The present is all there is. It is the space between past and future. It is the entryway and key to the future. The next activity stems from the present moment which may be a moment of observing, planning or other action. In flow, the task at hand absorbs the performer. Distractions are less likely to take the mind from them. Where is the activity? I don't see it.

Control is no problem. There is a strong sense of being in control while having a clear understanding of the limitations of one's control of his or her environment. Formal control and letting go are balanced so that control is no problem.

Formal control is analytically based; left brain. Letting go is the right brain in action—intuition, confidence coming through emersion in the present moment. In project work, project performance feedback is the foundation for formal control. We use the numbers but make decisions based on the combination of facts, experience and intuition. Control is no problem when it is an integral part of the process and the balance of right and left brain is right. Informed intuitive decisions replace knee jerk reaction and decision by numbers.

The sense of time is altered. This is a result or sign of flow as opposed to a condition for it. Time seems to go faster or slower. Sometimes what is hours seems like minutes, sometimes minutes seem like hours. This is only called *distortion* because we forget that the sense of time that comes from clocks and calendars is man made. In another sense, time is perceived subjectively. Time flies by or crawls. The clock is just ticking.

Absorption in the moment, concentration, is the condition that gives rise to the altered sense of time that indicates being in flow. In project work, there is often a sense that there isn't enough time. People may become anxious, cut corners, make errors. With the right frame of mind and reasonable controls one can let go into the performance and get the job done as perfectly as possible.

There is a *loss of ego.* This is another result of being in flow. When immersed in the work of the moment there is a loss of the subjective sense of self. One's problems and surroundings are forgotten. Don't worry, loss of ego is rarely permanent. The experience is conditioned on concentration and on mindfulness of our physical and mental movement from moment to moment. In project work as in any team activity the ability to join the flow of the team and its process enhances performance. In individual work, the loss of ego allows for the full power of intuition, training, knowledge and capacity to come through.

In the *Power of Full Engagement,* Jim Loehr and Tony Schwartz say that performance, health, and happiness come from the skillful management of energy. Full engagement is being in flow; being active and centered. "To be fully engaged, we must be physically energized, emotionally connected, mentally focused, and spiritually aligned with a purpose beyond our self interest."[67] The result is being focused, eager to get to work, and just as happy to return home to engage in non-work activity. We are in balance.

Knowing through Experience—Just Tasting

There are thousands of descriptions of being centered, in flow, present or fully engaged. They approximate a state that can only be really known through personal experience. Scientists are measuring the exact characteristics of the state. What they measure is the evidence of its effects, not the experience itself.

Sometimes a description will trigger an awareness of the experience itself. The words may match a feeling that you have known or describe one that you'd like to experience. They are not the experience itself. Just as the description of the taste of sugar is not the same as tasting sugar. Or, as the old Zen image of the reflection of the moon in a pond points out, don't get caught up in thinking that the reflection is the moon itself.

Do a little experiment. Taste something you really like (you can also use something you really dislike)—something sweet or salty, crunchy or soft. Note the initial taste sensation— salivation, shift of attention, bodily sensations … Note the moment that you began thinking about the taste, subtly commenting on it, wanting it to stay (or go away) forever. Try describing the taste itself. Did the taste and the commenting on it seem simultaneous, or was there a moment of just tasting?

The more we talk and think about it, the further we get from tasting; from being centered and in flow. In Zen we seek to experience each moment as a fertile, completely new stepping-off point to the future.

> How often have you faced a challenging situation and "lost it?"
> How often have you handled one really well? What was the difference in your experience? How did you feel?

The idea of *experiential knowing* is a major difference between mystical and intellectual views. The scientist who does not let go of his/her analytical thinking long enough to allow intuition to come to the surface fails to make the breakthrough discovery.

Perhaps everything is capable of being analytically proven, but why wait? Just now scientists are proving that meditation has a powerful effect on the mind and body that puts one in touch with powers of healing, physical performance, and mental excellence—inner resources that meditators and yogis have known and used for thousands of years

As was pointed out in the introduction, Zen is about "blowing the mind" out of its normal view. To really know, go beyond the intellect.

Question Beliefs

Knowing through experience is different than blind belief. When one knows that he is relaxed and focused and acting in a way that is completely in synch with the needs of the moment, helping, harming no one, in that moment there is a shift of consciousness. There is no need to believe anything. Belief is left-brain thinking; conditioning without proof; based on what others have experienced. It is habit. It is not an *authentic* experiencing of the moment.

In the Zen way, belief is unnecessary. One takes on a hypothesis and experiments to see if it is correct. The hypothesis is that being centered leads to performance excellence and breakthrough into full engagement, the flow experience. Mindfulness and concentration are the means to becoming centered. Ethical behavior and not harming others are the criteria used to test the results.

How to Be Centered—Technique

There are many techniques from many traditions across the world. They address the cultivation of concentration, ethical behavior, mindfulness, lovingkindness, and other positive qualities that are a means to becoming centered and to approach self-actualization.

The Zen practitioner combines wisdom, meditation, and ethical behavior to master herself, to self-actualize. The master practitioner operates without friction; naturally compassionate; unencumbered by the desire for things that cannot be; super-effective, always learning and opening.

Being centered is being behind the waterfall— calm, sitting behind the rush of the moment's events. The manager who can stay centered is more likely to be effective; to be responsive rather than reactive; to positively influence the outcome; to be able to dynamically balance all the continuums and paradoxes he or she has to work with.

Insight Meditation

The foundation method for becoming centered is the practice of insight or mindfulness meditation[68]. The method trains the mind. It increases the power of concentration while it cultivates the quality of the "observing mind" or mindfulness. This observing mind is found sitting behind all of our thoughts. Sometimes we are conscious of it; other times we are not. Regardless of our consciousness, it is always operating. It simply observes without judgment. The more subtle our awareness, the more we experience observing without identifying with the observer. There is mindfulness and awareness. They are just happening.

The insight practice leads to the sense that the observer is not in the head. We go beyond the egocentric, subjective way we habitually observe our environment to become truly objective—we, our thoughts, feelings, and physical sensations become objects in the field of awareness.

Insight Meditation Practice

Insight or mindfulness meditation can be practiced anytime and in any posture—sitting, standing, moving around, or lying down. Generally, when people think of meditation they think of sitting, often in a cross-legged posture, in a quiet and attractive place. There are great benefits from this kind of formal sitting meditation. They include increased concentration, de-stressing, and cultivating the awareness needed for presence in every moment. But, to limit meditation to formal sessions is a mistake. The point is to make everything you do a meditation on awareness.

Mindfulness

Mindfulness is paying attention in a non judgmental way with a mirror-like quality of mind. The mirror simply reflects. What is reflected does not change the mirror.

Joseph Goldstein, a Western teacher of Insight Meditation and co-founder of the Insight Meditation Society, says that "mindfulness is remembering the present object with the implication that the mind for that moment is free from attachment, aversion, and delusion."

Jon Kabot-Zinn, founder of Mindfulness-Based Stress Reduction said in an interview, "We often speak of mindfulness not just as bare attention but as affectionate attention. Woven into it is an orientation towards non-harming and seeing into the nature of things, which in some way implies, or at least invites, one to see the interconnectedness between the seer and the seen, the object and the subject."

Insight Meditation combines a cultivation of concentration with the cultivation of mindfulness. Concentration provides the ability to remember to be mindful. Mindfulness informs the mind that it is not concentrating.

The following practice is one variation on a theme. There are different practices for use as the meditator becomes more adept.

Sit comfortably erect. Head neck and back aligned. Shoulders hanging comfortably. Weight evenly distributed on your bottom. Hands where they are comfortable, for example folded in your lap or resting on your knees. Find a posture where you can sit quietly for awhile.

Take note of the sensations of your body – the pressure of your body against the seat, any tension, the feeling of the air around you on your skin, the temperature. Be aware of the sounds, smells, and sights around you. Be aware of your thoughts.

Either gently close your eyes or leave them open, if that is more comfortable. If your eyes are open, gaze downward without focusing on any particular object.

Relax.

Bring your attention to your breath. Find the breath at the nostrils or in the rising and falling of the abdomen or chest, wherever it is easiest to be aware of it. Use the breath as a touchstone. Come back to it whenever you become aware that you are lost in your thoughts and emotions.

Let your awareness include thoughts, emotional feelings, physical sensations, sights, sounds and smells. Simply observe them as they arise; note them. Bring your attention back to the breath.

At first, cultivate greater concentration and experience silence and calm by continuing to bring your attention back to the breath as soon as you realize that your attention has drifted to something else—thought, feeling, sensation. As you become more confident in your concentration, let go into the thoughts and feelings. Use each thought as the next point of attention.

When you find yourself lost in thoughts and emotions, bring your attention back to the breath. Note any tendency to become annoyed at being lost. The mind is being trained. Be patient, accepting, and firm.

Recognize each experience of *becoming aware of not being aware.* It is a special moment that strengthens the ability to be present and centered.

Continue. Bring the attention to the breath. Note thoughts and feelings. Become aware of being lost. Bring the attention back to the breath.

Managing Energy

We disengage from the day-to-day to recoup our energy. "… The key to expanding capacity is both to push beyond one's ordinary limits _and_ to regularly seek recovery, which is when growth actually occurs."[69] Sitting meditation is a means for recovery. Sitting meditation is a way to create a balance between active, outward-facing activity and inward-facing inactivity.

Sitting, though, is practice for meditation in the day-to-day world. Some meditation masters bring attention to the difference between meditating and being in meditation. To meditate is to actively engage in something. Someone, some aspect of mind is deciding to do it and doing it. Being in meditation is being in fully engaged flow. Meditation is happening. There is clarity, spaciousness, potential.

As this book has been saying, meditation can be applied anywhere that you can observe your thoughts, feelings, and sensations and be aware of your breath. In a meeting. Sitting at your desk. Walking down the street. Driving. Reading a book.

Here's how it works.

First you make a decision to practice. It's like a project. You have a goal, objectives and the need for effort and discipline.

Then, when you become aware that you are lost in your thoughts and emotions, bring your attention to a chosen point of reference— a "touchstone" that might be your breath or the sensations of your body. Become aware of your thoughts, senses, and emotions. Engage in what is going on around you, your work. When you become aware that you are lost in thoughts and emotions, bring your attention to your touchstone. Continue.

The more you practice, the less time you spend being lost in your thoughts and emotions. Being lost happens less frequently and for shorter periods of time. That means you are spending more time being centered. The more centered, the less stress and the lower the need for mental and emotional recovery. Physical recovery needs depend on the kind of physical activity you do. Mental and emotional recovery needs depend on how you perceive what you do.

As you practice mindfulness, you gain insights into the nature of your mind and the things that influence it. You see that things are impermanent because you observe them arise and pass away. You see the way that clinging operates. You confront your tendency to cling to "juicy" thoughts and push away unpleasant ones and strengthen your ability to change your mind. You see that there is no solid *I*.

Mindfulness meditation results in the strengthening of the witnessing aspect of mind. As the witness becomes more clearly active, the practitioner can more clearly see the difference between awareness and thinking. The multiple layers of the mind become clear.

In the first chapter, the technique of asking "Who am I?" was introduced. This question is subtly raised as mindfulness becomes stronger. Who is being mindful? Is mindfulness aware of being mindful? As the practice matures, the practitioner is mindful of awareness itself. The witness disappears and there is just witnessing, and then there is just awareness.

Are you aware of the part of your mind that is reading, reflecting on the content, aware of the reading and reflecting, aware of the awareness?

Being Centered and Being in Control

The difference between being centered and being "in control" is an important one to address. We've all been told to count to ten, or to bite one's lip, before speaking out of some emotion. These practices emulate being centered but differ because they often are associated with "stuffing" our feelings or swallowing our anger. We have the power to choose the response—a major step in the right direction—but, we haven't let the anger, or fear, or other emotion go. It stays on and may come out in other subtle and not so subtle ways.

When one is centered, the emotions arise and are acknowledged. With practice, they dissolve and no longer have the power to control one's behavior. They dissolve because we don't fuel them with our thoughts.

Being centered allows a project manager to differentiate between the right time to take action and the right time to allow the process to unfold and resolve itself. The balance between activity and passive acceptance is critical to success in managing anything. It is what allows the manager to avoid both micromanagement and under-managing in order to strike the right balance for the situation at hand. The right degrees of taking action, observing, directing, and using one's authority become clear. It becomes a natural part of the overall flow, instead of a reaction to one's need for control or reinforcement of one's own authority.

The right balance between rigid planning and allowing things to unfold also becomes clear. We understand that the plan is not deterministic. It is a guideline or set of control limits that give us direction. It does not dictate the way we must act. We are the ones who (with our co-stakeholders) decide how to act and what to change. We decide whether the plan is an accurate and useful guideline for project control and for predicting the outcome. If it is not, we decide to refine it or replace it.

Confidence in our ability to read and acknowledge the current situation gives us the ability to go with the flow, when that is appropriate, rather than attempt to redirect it. It also gives us the ability to redirect the flow when that is appropriate.

Systems and formal tools and techniques support and enhance this confidence. Managing against a plan using actual costs and effort, having a clear and documented understanding of the product and ultimate results, controlling changes and issues, addressing process issues, using appropriate tools—these are all skillful means to support project success and to create an environment that reflects the serenity at the center of it all.

Doing It—Changing Your Mind

A meditator, Susan, shared an experience in which she caught a ride to a two-week meditation retreat with someone who really annoyed her. For days, she found herself going over and over the annoyance, rehashing, planning for how she could have or should have dealt with it, why she was thinking about it and more.

After several days, Susan met with a meditation teacher and presented the problem. The teacher's advice was to imagine that she would soon be dying and decide whether she wanted to spend her remaining time dealing with this issue or moving on. The question jolted Susan and enabled her to stop fueling these thoughts. She observed them and brought her attention back to her breath. The obsessive thoughts did not immediately vanish, though they gradually lost their power and then disappeared.

Thinking has two parts, the initial thought and the development of that thought into a chain of thoughts, words, and actions. When we understand impermanence and our ability to cultivate a mind that can eliminate the gasping that causes us to suffer, we are motivated to make the effort to change our thinking.

When a thought arises, sometimes, simply noticing it will allow it to dissipate, moving across the mind as a cloud moves across the sky. Other times the thought will stay for a while. When it is there, we have the opportunity to apply the power of concentration to eliminate it. We can replace it with another thought. Or we can choose to follow it.

If an angry wave of thought fills the mind, instead of justifying the anger, or indulging in righteous anger, replace it with thoughts of compassion or focus strongly on any object.

As the thought wave reappears over and again, gently but firmly go back to the new thought. Break the wave, soften its power, and let it go. The earlier in the sequence the remedy is applied, the more quickly it works.

The hard part is the resolve and discipline to let go of the current thought. Giving up the pleasure or comfort or need to hold on to the current thought is hard work. Here is where we learn to cut through our clinging, and by doing so become free.

Recap

Why do we want to cultivate clarity and quiet? For two reasons: 1) to continuously improve performance and 2) to approach self-actualization.

Being *centered, in flow,* and *present* all express the experience of being in touch with our foundation or core. When we are experiencing a clear and quiet state we can be objective, in dynamic balance between the extremes in all things, responsive rather than reactive, peaceful and powerful; able to act or not act in complete harmony with the present moment.

This experience can be cultivated. We make everything a meditation by bringing attention back to the present moment, using the breath or physical sensations as a touchstone when we recognize that we are <u>lost</u> in thoughts or reactive emotions.

Being centered is more about letting than doing. It is said that the more we try, the further we go away from our center. When we rest in the present we become increasingly aware of what is and has been there all along.

Of course, there is always paradox—if there is no goal or intention and no effort there is no gain. When we exercise right effort for the right intention we cultivate the art of doing while not doing.

What's Next

Taking the heart of this book into action is the next step. The theme of doing the inner and outer work simultaneously is a critical part of the Zen approach.

The outer work is about applying knowledge and concrete skills to the perfection of the form. If you are managing projects make sure you have the knowledge and skill to effectively initiate, plan, execute, monitor and control, and close projects. That means knowing how to set and manage expectations by defining scope and realistically estimating and scheduling; how to communicate solid information about the state of the project to enable accurate assessment and continuous adjustment of the plan; how to use the right tools; and how to close the project effectively.

> **Patrol Rimpoche, in *The Words of My Perfect Master,* says "While having every intention to study and practice Dharma[70], you may well keep putting it off until tomorrow or the next day, day by day all of your life. You must avoid a whole lifetime of planning to practice."**

The inner work is done as the outer work is being done. Here the critical next step is to take stock of the state of your mind and the mental models that underlie the way you behave. Do you have a process perspective? Do you consciously work at self-actualization and continuous improvement? Do you cultivate responsiveness? Are you mostly centered or are you caught in the waterfall?

The simplest (not necessarily easy) way to take action is to begin a meditation practice to increase concentration and mindfulness. There are two components, formal practice and continuous practice in daily life.

Formal practice is done by choosing a specific time and place and meditating for a predetermined period of time. Pick a place that is comfortable and relatively quiet. Arrange things so that you won't be interrupted. There is no need for any props or special equipment. You can sit in a chair or on a cushion. You can sit for ten or fifteen minutes to start and then increase to 30 minutes to an hour. Be disciplined but remember to enjoy the experience.

Formal practice is a foundation for the continuous practice in daily life. It is very effective but not absolutely necessary. Practice in daily life is where the real work is, remembering to come back to the present when lost in reactive thought and behavior.

As the practice matures you will experience its fruits— calm clarity. You will become free of reactive behavior, naturally compassionate, and far more capable of effective performance than you have ever been.

> **Are you awake? Are you sure? Who is asking? Who is responding?**

Appendix I
How to Manage Projects—
The Basics

> **Looking with the eye of an expert, one is conditioned by past experience. Looking at things like a beginner, there is a continuous, fresh and open attitude.**

This appendix describes the underlying principles, concepts, and techniques of project management (PM), and reaffirms its goal—to improve the probability of a project's success. Here we define terms; identify roles, critical activities and skills; and create a systematic framework for understanding the process of PM.

Even if you are already familiar with PM as a formal discipline, you may find this review useful, and a source of new insights. Reviewing the basics is always a valuable way to remind oneself of best practices and how everything fits together. When working with complex processes like project management, people often get lost in the details. Each time we review the fundamentals in the light of experience, we get a deeper understanding of their real meaning and subtlety. Going back to general principles, we notice things that clear away obstacles and turn on light bulbs.

Many people begin managing projects long before they are aware of any systematic approach. If you have been managing projects intuitively, or by the seat-of-your-pants, it will be useful to have a comprehensive sense of PM as a systematic process. Even if you find that it's just mostly good sense, and what you have already been doing all along, you'll have the added benefit of doing it consciously, with intention.

Another benefit of going back to basics is that it puts everyone involved in a project on the same page. Most projects are joint efforts. That is why a common language and shared processes are such critical success factors. If the people you do projects with—your associates (peers, superiors and subordinates, vendors, clients, and others)—all use different terminology and have different ways of doing the same things, you will waste time on avoidable problems and miss the chance to continuously improve.

An Approximation of the Real Process

But do not *mindlessly* follow any defined project management process. Because of the human element and the vast number of variables, project management is complex. Any definition of a complex process is an approximation.

Still, by defining the process, you gain insight into its subtle workings and unstated assumptions and beliefs. You become aware of concepts and techniques not otherwise obvious and can now apply them to overcome barriers. Even if you are "doing it right" already, your confidence is tested and reinforced by seeing that what you are doing is a defined process that has been tested by others.

> The Buddha was very clear in advising his students not to take his teachings as beliefs. Accept them, he said, only when you know from personal experience that they are true.

Project management, like Zen, is not based on beliefs or fixed models of behavior. It is a scientific exploration of experience in the context of a model. The practitioner tests the model and creatively adapts it to current conditions, making use of accumulated wisdom and collective experience.

Why do it your own way if there is a better way, or one that is just as good that everyone else around you is already using? Conversely, why do it someone else's way if it doesn't suit your situation?

What a Project Is

A project is a temporary effort to achieve objectives within time and cost constraints. It ends when its objective(s) are met or when those with the authority to, decide to end it. To meet objectives means to deliver an outcome (that is, a new or changed product, service, process, or event) with defined quality, within time and cost constraints, to the satisfaction (if not delight) of the sponsors, clients, and other stakeholders[71]. Projects are finite; often they are referred to as "objective oriented work." Operational activities are those ongoing processes like billing, customer help, and other administrative tasks. While operational activities are repetitive, every project is unique, to at least some degree. Many operational activities, in turn, are made up of a series of projects.

What Project Management Is

> "The most successful men in the end are those whose success is the result of steady accretion... It is the man who carefully advances step by step, with his mind becoming wider and wider—and progressively better able to grasp any theme or situation—persevering in what he knows to be practical, and concentrating his thought upon it, who is bound to succeed in the greatest degree."
> Alexander Graham Bell[72]

Project management is "the application of knowledge, skills, tools, and techniques to project activities in order to meet or exceed stakeholder needs and expectations from a project."[73] PM applies principles and techniques to the initiation, planning, execution, control, and completion of projects, and adds value by improving the likelihood of success.

Although project management and project performance are always integrated, they are two distinct operations. Performance is the means to outcome; management is the means to effective performance, ensuring that the probability of success is high. Generally, about 90 percent of the work effort is spent on performance and 10 percent on managing. Another important difference is that, while project performance is specific to each project, project management principles and techniques can be applied across projects.

Balancing Flexibility and Discipline

Project management may be done more or less formally. *Formally* means putting project understandings (such as plans, decisions, objectives, requirements definitions, and change requests) in writing, clearly defining roles and responsibilities to promote accountability and following a pre-established, repeatable process. Formality connotes the disciplined (especially <u>self</u>-disciplined) use of practices that add value. Too little formality leads to chaos and waste; too much to bureaucracy and waste.

Project management is not a discipline in the sense of dealing with children's behavior or meting out punishment, but in the sense of self-control in a specific context. Discipline implies following a set of principles in a process. Scientists, engineers and other professionals all have disciplines; artists have disciplines. An antonym of *discipline* is *chaos.*

All disciplines work similarly. If the rules are too rigid, there won't be enough room for the adaptations people need to make to succeed. For example, if you follow a strict rule regardless of the situation about the amount of paperwork there should be, there will very likely be either too much or not enough. Project managers must be able to adapt or tailor project management to the type (based on the number of participants, budget, duration, subject area, complexity, among other criteria) of the project being performed. Formality without flexibility leads to bureaucracy, and in today's fast moving, fast- changing world, bureaucracy is too costly and too slow. But flexibility without enough formality is chaotic, and chaos is also costly, as well as inefficient.

> "To adapt means to bring an organism into correspondence with the reality of a situation—that is, to creatively adjust, reconcile and fit. To be adaptable is to be pliable, supple, tractable, and moldable."
>
> David H. Shuster[74]

Balancing formality and flexibility allows for creativity, adaptation to undefined situations, and continuous improvement, while maintaining a clearly stated set of standards, procedures, and guidelines that promote best practices.

Systems View

To understand projects and project management most effectively, we take a systems view. This view is intrinsic to Zen, which assumes the underlying interconnectedness of all things. In the systems view, everything (things, people, organizations, events, and processes) interact and operate in a system. The system is like a black box that takes in some inputs and produces outputs. In addition, each system exists within a higher order system, like a set of nested boxes. Any change or activity within or around the system can affect another part of the system, or the way the system as a whole behaves.

The more one can predict the impact of activity in a system, the greater one's control of its performance. In complex systems, no one can ever predict the effect of actions with 100 percent accuracy. A project is a complex system. Project management, too, is a complex system that operates both inside and outside of the project itself. The better the map of the system, its higher level system (its environment) and its subsystems (its subprojects, teams, etc.) the more likely it is that we can predict the impact of actions on the system and its environment.

For example, the impact of a member of the project team leaving can be more easily and accurately assessed if there is a clear understanding of what that person was doing, his status, what he was supposed to do in the future, why he was the one assigned (e.g., he might have been the only one with the required skills), and who he was in contact with.

PM as a System

Figure 1, below, describes the project management process. International Institute for Learning (IIL)'s Unified Project Management Methodology (UPMM™) describes the various activities involved in the management of single or multiple projects, as well as the management of the process itself. These activities are performed by people (human resources, in corporate PM speak). They use other resources—such as machines, facilities and supplies) to produce outcomes.

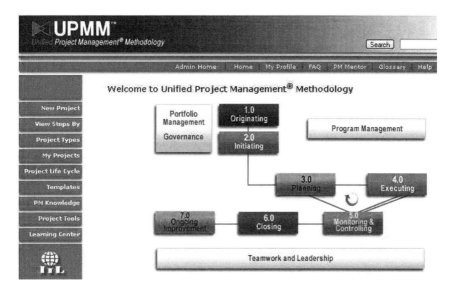

Figure 1: Project management as a system[75]

Referring to the diagram in figure 1, Governance, is the process that covers Portfolio Management to select the right projects, provide the right procedures, policies, tools, and standards, and ensure that the right resources are effectively organized and available.

Project management begins well before a project becomes a project. A single project is managed from Originating (step 1.0 in figure 1), the time someone communicates an idea that may someday become a project, through Closing (step 6.0), the completion of the project, if in fact the project becomes a project and is completed. Originating may entail a sales process and/or a work request evaluation/project selection process. Originating is as much a part of portfolio management[76] as it is part of the management of individual projects.

In most cases there are multiple projects performed both simultaneously and serially. Ongoing improvement (step 7.0 in figure 1) involves evaluation of the results of multiple projects to continuously improve performance by refining the PM and project performance processes. Connecting these processes is collaboration and consulting. And the foundation of effective collaboration is Communication—candid, complete, clear, mutually understood, and controlled. Communication is the critical factor that gives project stakeholders the ability to negotiate, plan, motivate, solve problems, keep one another informed, and reach consensus.

Project Management Activities

Managing a project means performing the activities necessary to ensure that:

- The project is initiated for the right reasons by the right people in the right way.
- Goals, objectives and acceptance criteria are defined and mutually understood by all parties.
- Requirements are defined (usually in cycles of progressively detailed definitions).
- A plan is developed to state how the involved people and groups will carry out the project under the expected budget and schedule, with a clear understanding of the degree of risk and uncertainty involved.
- Resources are available when they are needed.
- Work is performed according to the plan, and/or the plan is

changed to coincide with real performance and realistic projections to completion.

- The project is on the right track and is still worth doing.
- Interested parties are kept abreast of project performance and projections to completion.
- Bills are paid and files of documents maintained.
- The final result is acceptable and passed on to those who will manage and use it after the project is over.
- The project is used as a learning experience to provide feedback into the PM process.

These activities are summed up in the major processes of Originating; Initiating; Planning; Executing; Monitoringand Controlling; Closing, and Ongoing Improvement, as shown in figure 1, above.

These activities are performed in a *nonlinear* process. For example, planning the project requires people to spend time and money and is therefore part of project execution and needs to be monitored and controlled. Requirements must be defined, estimates made, and risks assessed, to some degree. These are all planning activities. Planning is also performed iteratively during the project as requirements are defined and refined as events occur in levels of detail that change the premises underlying the plan.

Project Success, Products and Objectives

A successful project meets its objectives. It delivers a desired outcome on time and within budget. It fulfills the needs of its stakeholders—project sponsors, clients, users of the product, managers, support people, project performers, and all others who have a vested interest in the project and its outcome. Project sponsors and users should be satisfied that the project's results add value. A project may be considered successful—even if it is canceled when it becomes clear that to continue it will cost more than the results will be worth.

A product or outcome is the result of a project. It might be a new or upgraded product, a renovated business process, or an event or service offering. Product success depends on the usefulness and/or marketability of the product, typically with regard to reducing operating costs, improving customer service, making a profit, gaining pleasure, or avoiding risk and pain, among the other goals that have justified performing the project. The fact that a project successfully produces a product on time and within budget does *not* by itself fulfill the promise that led to the initiation of the project. What if the product was no longer marketable, because a more advanced technology had been developed or a new process was implemented but failed to make work more effective? You've probably heard the old joke: *"The operation was a success but the patient died."*

Business objectives describe the reasons the project is being performed, while project objectives describe the desired outcome of the project itself. Business objectives refer to product success. Project objectives define the criteria for project success. Project objectives should be measurable, linked to strategic initiatives, prioritized with respect to one another and the objectives of other projects, and clearly understood by project stakeholders.

Objectives should be expressed in levels of detail. A concise statement, limited to a few objectives, is more likely to be understood and accepted than a long list. These major objectives may then be subdivided into more detailed objectives.

Project Management Tools

Project management tools fall into three categories: PM Information Systems (PMIS), collaboration tools, and knowledge management tools. PMIS tools assist in scheduling, recording, and managing project information and in reporting. Collaboration tools support communication and cooperation among project participants. Knowledge management tools provide process definitions, templates and checklists and guide and assist performers in doing their work.

Remember: Tools don't do the work, they make the work easier to do—if people know how to use them correctly. Don't think that if you buy Microsoft Project it will do your scheduling for you. If you don't know how to create a nicely structured list of tasks that identifies all the work to be performed, you may end up with a schedule that looks good but is totally misleading.

The Keys to Success—People

Projects are performed by people, and the human factor is by far the most complex and critical. Don't think a spiffy project management tool or even a comprehensive cookbook of policies, procedures and templates is going to solve problems rooted in interdepartmental warfare, lack of effective communication, illogical problem solving and decision making, fear and blame-based politics and the other common causes of project performance ills.

Look to group dynamics, communication skills, and the problem-solving process. Look to adaptability and the ability to manage continuous change in a nonlinear system. These are where the keys to successful project management lie.

Spiral Progression to an End

While we can identify the steps in managing a project, they are not as discretely separate and linear as they seem. A project is fluid. It moves naturally from stage to stage in a progression of increasingly detailed understandings of what is to be done, why it is to be done, whether it should be done, and how it is to be done.

Depending on the subject, setting, size, complexity and criticality of a project, there may be several points at which decisions are made to continue or end a project. Performing the project is relatively straightforward if the understandings that come from the work of originating, initiating, and planning are effectively handled.

Detailed requirements are progressively defined and estimates are iteratively refined during originating, initiating, and planning to enable incremental decision-making and funding. This protects project sponsors and clients from unnecessary expenditures caused by run-away projects. And it protects project performers and their managers from having to make definitive estimates without the right information about factors that influence the estimate.

Change is a fact of life in projects—people, objectives, requirements and conditions all change. Change control (handling change within the project) and change management (directing and handling the effects of change in the project environment) are critical parts of project management.

Project Management Processes and Areas of Knowledge

Let's drill down a bit into the process of project management by defining each of the processes identified in figure 1 above: Originating; Initiating; Planning; Executing; Monitoring and Controlling; Closing; and Ongoing Cross-Project Improvement.

According to the PMI PMOBK® Guide, nine areas of knowledge are applied across the process. These areas of knowledge are integration, scope management, time management, cost management, communications management, human resource management, quality management, risk management, and procurement (contracts) management.

Originating

Originating is the set of activities that turns a potential project—an idea, opportunity or a possible sale—into a project. Originating may be a sales process that culminates in a contract to perform project work. Or it may be the process of vetting ideas and work requests to filter out those that are deemed valuable enough to be worth the effort of fleshing out their description and creating proposal or decision documents for the initiation process.

In service organizations like consultancies, projects are sold to satisfy client needs. Engagement management is the process that encompasses sales, project management, customer service, and delivery in these organizations. Originating is as much a part of the sales process as the project management process.

In organizations like in-house maintenance and support groups, originating may be part of a change and issues management process. In a Six Sigma context, originating is part of the quality management effort. In product development, originating is part of the new product idea vetting process.

During originating, the idea is identified, described, and evaluated to determine if it is a candidate project. If it is, the idea is transformed into a "proposal" that then becomes the input to the initiating process. Very high-level descriptions of the project objectives and outcome and rough estimates, which can be expressed with fairly wide ranges of cost and time possibilities, are provided. These estimates are based on one or more strategies for how the project would be carried out and a documented list of constraints, assumptions, and risks.

In some settings, originating and initiating flow together, while in other, more formal settings, there is a distinct division between them.

Initiating

During project origination and initiation you define the project's business objectives (the principal reasons for performing the project) and project outcome. You define the outcome in terms of its characteristics (features, functions, and performance criteria). You also refine cost, time, and other constraints, assess risk, and identify the scope of, and key participants in, the project.

Note that in general, there is *no* clear boundary between originating and initiating. The definition of the project that results from originating and initiating is the beginning of the detailed project definition that will be refined throughout the project's life as changes are identified and applied. During this phase, individual organizations may identify specific documents and procedures an idea or possibility has to go through to become a project.

Project scope includes the definition of the project outcome, the work to be performed, and the breadth of impact and involvement of people and organizations. It is defined progressively across originating, initiating and planning processes. The scope is refined throughout the project.

The project is initiated when the appropriate authorities determine if the desired outcome warrants the time, effort, risk, and resources necessary to produce the product. In formal settings, a Project Charter is created to document the understandings regarding the project and to officially authorize work to begin. It is a best practice in any setting to write a concise (one to three page) description of the project that clearly identifies objectives, participants, outcomes, risks, constraints and assumptions. If there is a contract between project performers and the project client, the charter should be a summary of the contract.

Initiation may be a relatively short process or one that is extended over time and performed iteratively as the product and its costs and expected benefits are further defined in detail. Work may be incrementally authorized, at checkpoints, to obtain greater assurance that assumptions and the estimates based on them are correct before committing time, money, and other resources.

Originating and initiating are also part of portfolio management. Since projects always occur in environments where other things (projects, operational activities) are going on, it is wise to consider how the individual project will affect and be affected by them. For example, since resources are almost always limited, what trade-offs and priorities will have to be made among projects competing for them?

Planning

Planning begins when the idea for a project is first stated and someone provides a rough estimate of how much it would cost or how long it would take to actualize the idea. That means that planning overlaps with originating and initiating the project.

Through planning we ensure that results are in keeping with expectations, and that work efforts are efficiently and effectively performed. Planning identifies the way the project will be performed, who will perform it, when interim and final results will be ready, how much risk and uncertainty there is, and how to deal with it, how much the plan is subject to variance, how many of what kinds of resources will be needed and when, and how much the project will cost.

> The objective of planning is to get a realistic sense of what it will take to deliver the project outcome. Anyone can create a "plan" to do anything in any amount of time for any amount of money. The challenge is to create a plan that accurately reflects the way the project will unfold.

The result of planning is a project plan. It consists of:

- Business and project objectives
- A description of the outcome and its acceptance criteria
- A structured list of tasks or activities, also known as a work breakdown structure or wbs, with descriptions of each activity, including its outcome(s), dependencies with other tasks, resource requirements, the people assigned and effort and duration estimates
- A schedule
- A budget
- Role and responsibility assignments
- Standards and procedures for how the project will be managed and performed.

Planning is performed throughout the life of a project. Iterative plan refinement uses the information that results from an increasingly detailed description of the product and from project control. Confidence in the plan's accuracy increases as assumptions are proven by actual experience. As earlier assumptions are proven to be erroneous, need for re-planning is identified.

Planning is the central process group and the most complex. It is described in more detail in the next topics covering the major parts of planning:

- Defining Scope
- Work Breakdown/Task Analysis
- Estimating and Scheduling and the Triple Constraints
- Sequencing
- Resources
- Optimizing
- Risk and Uncertainty
- Limiting the Workload—Saying No

Defining Scope. Scope refers to the outcome of the project, that is, to the product in terms of its "features and functions," and to the overall work to be performed. Scope includes a definition of the impact and nature of the project's setting. For example, the project's setting may be within a global organization but the scope of its impact may be local to a particular division or region.

The scope definition requires effort and time; it could take weeks or months to accomplish. Scope definition consists of describing the project's context and overall goals and objectives, requirements definition and design. Scope definition starts with the overall understanding of what the project is to deliver and under what conditions. For example: "The project will result in a party for 150 people to celebrate the December holiday season at a location near the office for no more than $100.00 per person."

Requirements definition drills down into the details. Some of the details might include the need for fish and vegetarian dishes, alcohol (or not), music, space for dancing, decorations to represent all the religious and cultural traditions of the group.

Design describes how the requirements are to be met. In our example the design might include selection of the location, decoration specifications, menu and bar selections.

The quality of the outcome must be defined at each level of the scope definition.

The goal of scope definition is to make sure that stakeholders, particularly sponsors, clients and performers, share a common understanding of what the project will deliver. The scope definition becomes the criteria that will be used to determine if the project's results are acceptable. The definition directs the project performers.

Work Breakdown/Task Analysis. Based on the project's scope, the planners identify and describe the work to be performed as a set of tasks or activities. This creates a foundation for the rest of project. While the desired outcome drives the project, it is the work that is the focus of estimating, scheduling, and controlling performance.

The work breakdown structure (WBS) is a structured task list. The main "trick" in identifying tasks is to provide levels of detail, beginning with a few high level activities that represent <u>all</u> the work needed to meet the objectives of the project. You then break each of these down into a few activities that represent the work needed to accomplish each one. If the activities at this level are longer than a week or two in duration, break each of them, in turn, down into a few activities and continue until you have identified all the work at a level of detail that is meaningful and useful for estimating, scheduling, and controlling the project.

This breaking down (*decomposition* is the term used by the pros) of the work can be done over time for large complex projects or all at once for smaller and simpler ones. Often, it isn't possible to identify all of the work needed for developing the product until the work of defining it has been done.

Some readers may be thinking that this sounds like a lot of work, and that they'll end up with lots of tasks to manage. Actually it is not so difficult and is made much easier if there are standard task lists or if old project plans are used as a base. Standard task lists and the use of old project plans make use of the similarity of many, if not most projects, to ones previously performed. The first holiday party becomes a template for the planning of all the subsequent ones.

As for there being lots of tasks, that is an advantage when it comes time to figure out how much time and effort the project will take. It is also an advantage when trying to control the project; it's the base that gives everyone a sense of what has been done and what is left to be done. Think about how nice it would be to be able to see clearly every so often whether progress has really been made; not because someone says so but because there is clear evidence of accomplishment.

Estimating and Scheduling and the Triple Constraints. In every project there are three primary constraints or objectives—the outcome, time, and cost. The outcome is represented by the scope definition, the time is the desired delivery date, and the cost constraint is the budget. Realism in project planning means estimating the work to be done so that there is a strong likelihood that the outcome will be delivered when and for the price expected. Project managers are expected to "push back" when faced with a desired target date that is unrealistic and based on factors outside the project (e.g., the conditions in the marketplace, desire for greater profit or reduction of expenses, legal regulations, etc.). The triangle representing the triple constraints must be real, not imaginary.

> It is better to know in advance whether something can be done than it is to find out at the last minute, when everyone is anxiously expecting the outcome.

Even though a target date may be stated as a directive—"It must be done by this date"—wise project managers know that it should be interpreted as a question: "Can we deliver an acceptable outcome by the date?" The same is true of the desired budget. It is an objective or constraint. It is best to put these targets aside for the moment and focus in on what it will take to deliver the desired outcome, given the most likely conditions. Then, the project manager is in a position to negotiate realistic expectations.

> *Most likely* **is not to be confused with what everyone would most like to have happen. It refers to what will probably happen under normal conditions.**

The basic principles of effective estimating and scheduling are to 1) base the estimates on past experience and expert knowledge as much as possible, 2) recognize that estimates are not actual results and therefore there is uncertainty, 3) assess and plan for uncertainty, 4) base schedules on a logical flow or sequence of the work, 5) base estimates and schedules on realistic expectations regarding the availability of resources (people, machines, facilities and supplies), and 6) not expect the plan to be right the first time and engage in refining and optimizing it by playing what-if games that identify different scope definitions, cost possibilities, time frames, scenarios, sequences, and application of resources.

Unfortunately, project management tools do not estimate or sequence project activities, and they do not know the project resources; nor do they do a very good job of automatically scheduling and rescheduling even after they are given estimates, sequences, and resource information. Estimating the project cost and schedule requires knowledge of the work to be done and of the resources to do it. The knowledge comes from the past experience of project planners or from data collected in past projects. If there are many similar projects, keep records of past project performance and use them in estimating future ones. This data takes the form of prototypical project task lists with task sequences identified and past cost and duration results. However, it is important to carefully account for differences between past projects and those being estimated. Remember, while things repeat, they don't repeat in exactly the same way.

> Each project is like a snowflake. From afar it looks like all the other snowflakes. Close up, it is unique.

Sequencing. Sequencing is a very important part of planning. It is in sequencing that the activities are analyzed to determine the best logical flow of one to the next. That flow is based on dependencies (the relationships among activities, particularly, which ones need to be completed before others can be performed). Many project planners do not spend enough time analyzing these dependency relationships among the activities and end up with plans that are either overly optimistic—because they assume that activities can be done in parallel when in fact they cannot—or pessimistic, because they do not take advantage of those activities that can be done in parallel.

> Optimism is great, though when planning a project it is better to be realistic—not optimistic, not pessimistic.

Resources. Without resources, no work gets done. Above we mentioned the triple constraints that are put on the project by the client ("I want this product, by this time for this price"). Resources represent another constraint, one imposed by the project's environment. To estimate and schedule a project realistically you must consider the capability and availability of the resources.

Have you ever hired a contractor who estimated that a job would take three months and then disappeared for days at a time to work on other jobs, making yours take five months? If you have, you know that assuming resources will be available when they are not leads to unfulfilled expectations.

Planning requires a realistic assessment of whether staff and other resources will be available at the right time. Do not assume that people who are working on multiple tasks while they are assigned to your project will be available 100 percent of their time. And do not assume that projects using resources assigned to your project that are supposed to end before your project needs the resources will actually end. Make it a part of your planning to assess the likelihood of the resources being there when you expect them.

In addition to the availability of resources, their quality is important. Human resources have a range of capabilities—some are experts, others, novices; and while some experts really are expert, others are in name only. Some are able to work well with others while others are challenged in their ability to collaborate and communicate. Estimating and scheduling requires an assessment of the quality of the resources.

> Remember, project management tools help to make sequencing and evaluating resource requirements easier, but knowledgeable people do the estimating and scheduling.

Optimizing. In order to have both a realistic plan and one that makes the best use of resources, the plan is optimized to come to the right combination of outcome, cost, and time with the client and/or sponsor deciding on priorities among these triple constraints. This means that the outcome, target date, budget, available resources, tools and techniques and the project environment may all be adjusted to find a realistic and optimum plan to achieve objectives. Remember, pushing back and justifying why you may have to say no is part of the process of managing expectations and ensuring project success.[77]

> The only thing that is certain is uncertainty.

Assessing Risk and Uncertainty. After identifying events that might upset the plan or opportunities that might make it more likely to be achieved, planners identify actions that could make the negative less probable, or have less impact, while promoting the opportunities. They develop contingency plans and reserves to protect stakeholders from false expectations and unacceptable losses.

Note the connection between identifying, analyzing, and accommodating risk and expectations. If stakeholders do not look at risk and uncertainty realistically they may expect outcomes to be more certain than they actually are.

Once risk and uncertainty are acknowledged as inevitable, it is possible to manage them. Managing risk involves identifying and assessing it, planning to handle it before and after it affects the project, and planning how it will be handled in the project. For those risks that cannot be "planned away," contingency plans and reserves can be created to make the project plan more realistic and performance more effective.

Limiting the Workload. Saying "no" or at least "not now" is a major prerequisite for effective project planning. People are overwhelmed by an unlimited flow of work. Saying no to clients and senior managers who make what they see as reasonable and necessary demands and requests is *not* easy.

Yet, to really satisfy clients and management and to successfully grow and survive as a person or organization, there must be a reasonable flow of work, <u>not</u> a flood. Floods lead to constant priority shifts and overwork, which in turn lead to an inability to fulfill commitments to deliver quality products within time and cost constraints. Late and poor quality products cost—both in money and customer confidence. And constant overwork costs the organization in burn-out and high turnover of the most valuable people.

There are thousands of ways to say no creatively. Among the more effective are: "Your deadline is understandable. Let's see how we can work together to free up the resources to get it done. " "It would be great to be able to deliver the product for that price in that schedule. Let's see what features we can eliminate to make it possible. " These tend to lead to more successful outcomes than "Are you joking!? " or "There's no way."

An effective portfolio management process, in which senior decision makers assess the priority of projects and the availability and capability of resources to accomplish them, makes it less necessary for individual project managers to have to say "no."

Executing, Monitoring, and Controlling

To keep interested people abreast of project performance and manage their expectations, you have to monitor performance against the plan and control changes and issues. Control of changes refers to the handling of requests for changes to, say, the requirements or scope of the project. Without change control there is a tendency for the project to unconsciously grow beyond its original scope.

Data is collected to evaluate progress and plan ongoing refinement and improvement. Project control consists of *progress* control, *information* control, *quality* control, *change* control and *issues* control.

In fact, most of the labor in project management is expended on controlling. It is necessary to scale the controlling to the needs of the project. Over-controlling wastes time and money. Under-controlling creates unnecessary risk and fails to manage expectations.

While there is a school of thought that says formal project control is a waste of time, it is the collective opinion of wise project managers that objective reporting of what has and hasn't been done, and what that means regarding a project's expected completion, is a critical part of the process.

Progress control collects data and reports on compliance with the schedule and budget. The data are task completions, effort and cost expenditures by task, and the occurrence and cause of any variances between actual performance and the plan. Variance is the difference between the planned and actual outcome of the project. The longer and more complex the project and the more uncertain project sponsors are about its nature, the greater the potential variance.

Periodic reports, clearly and candidly giving the status of the project with respect to the plan, are used to decide if any redirection is needed. Progress control and reporting can be as simple as reports showing expected vs. actual completion of tasks, or as sophisticated as Earned Value analysis and other techniques to show integrated data regarding budget and schedule performance. Based on variances, the project team decides how best to respond and refine the plan—for example, to work faster or smarter, or to accept the situation and change the expected target dates and budgets.

Information control regulates the flow of communication and maintains the documentation that describes the product and the project process. Requirements definitions, designs, marketing materials, training materials, and other materials in any media from hard copy to videos make up the product documentation. The plan, status reports, issues and resolutions, and changes and their disposition make up project process documentation. Communication includes reporting, problem and issues resolution, and the exchange of information among project stakeholders to execute the project.

Quality control assesses the acceptability of both interim results and the final product. Interim results are assessed to catch errors and omissions as early as possible in order to reduce their impact on the project.

Change control manages the changes that are inevitably made to the definition of the objectives, product definition, and plan. The goal is to minimize disruptions to project performance by postponing as many changes as possible. Uncontrolled change in product specifications is a primary cause of schedule and budget overruns. Note that postponing or avoiding making changes is a means for improving the probability of getting the project done on time and within budget. Some changes must be made during the project, while others can be postponed and still others never have to be made. For example, a newly requested feature to a product may be very desirable but adding it might delay the completion of the product as originally envisioned by several weeks or months. The new feature could be added later after the product has been delivered in the context of a product enhancement project.

The decision to make, postpone, or reject requested changes is made by stakeholders who are determined at the project's onset to be the change authorities. They decide based on the reason for the change and the change's predicted impact on the project.

Issues control records issues and problems as they arise and ensures that they are addressed by assigning them to responsible people and tracking their progress. Issues may include questions regarding any aspect of the product or project. Their resolution may result in changes to the project plan and/or the product definition.

Closing

Projects end when the client and others accept that project objectives have been achieved or when people in authority decide to terminate. In most projects, closing implies a transition from the project to operations in which the project's results are used for their intended purpose. This transition is one of the most delicate aspects of the project. The right people must be trained and left with the ability to effectively use and support the product. In addition, there should be a method for determining the effectiveness of the product over its life, which often is far longer than the life of the project.

Resources, human and other, must be redeployed, but not until all the work is done. Work to perform the transition and to offer some ongoing support may be necessary and there may be cleanup. In formal settings, budget lines must be formally closed and the documentation that represents the project history and product description must be archived.

Finally, a post implementation review should be held to assess the success of the project and highlight lessons learned to improve the performance of future projects.

Ongoing Improvement—Learning from Experience

Organizations learn in much the same way people do. That is why Project management includes a learning process. Each project is an experience organizations can draw on for learning how to perform the next project more effectively. Evaluate performance periodically throughout the project and upon its completion and then publish the results to inform others of the pitfalls and best practices you discovered. Over time, best practices are carried forward, poor practices are discarded, and estimates become increasingly accurate because they are based on past experience.

This learning happens on a project by project basis by collecting lessons learned, and across multiple projects by evaluating and learning from trends.

Note that some project management cultures are *learning disabled,* while others truly recognize the value of spending the time and effort to evaluate performance and really make use of the results. To obtain the value of improved performance requires an investment of time and effort for project performance reviews and the capture of lessons learned in project plans and budgeting for cross-project improvement efforts.

Accountability But Not Blaming

The culture that supports an effective project management process must value and promote clear accountability. Project management principles require that commitments be made and documented and that status with respect to those commitments be reported with *compassionately ruthless* candor and regularity—nothing is hidden.

> Compassionately ruthless: Be ruthless by addressing even the most uncomfortable issues, like poor performance by individuals or groups. Be compassionate by recognizing the sensitivity often required where there is candid criticism and focusing on causes and solutions rather than blame.

Replace blaming with acceptance, coupled with a disciplined analysis of cause to promote continuous improvement. Cultivate teamwork by rewarding people for overall project success as well as success in their own activities; continuously reinforce team values; and remind people of the big picture and the need for collaborative efforts. Expand role definitions to include partnering with others and not just working as individuals.

Project Management—A Value Adding Discipline

If you want better project results, mange your projects better.

Project management is a process that adds value by ensuring that the "right" projects are done in the "right" way. It promotes realistic schedules and budgets. It leads to lower costs and shorter schedules by promoting best practices across projects, while eliminating the repetition of known errors and omissions. It makes estimating more accurate and easier. And it gives stakeholders clear, concise, and accurate information about project status and the prognosis for completion.

To quantify the value of project management, identify the costs of project overruns, poor quality products, chronic overtime, and the other symptoms of poorly managed projects. Then track the way that more effective project management practices change performance and eliminate unnecessary costs and delays. Include an assessment of the improvement of relationships among project stakeholders and how much that is worth in the long run. While this is hard to quantify, it must be highly valued, as it is the foundation for all performance.

Implementing project management disciplines in an organization requires a concerted effort over a protracted period of time. The difficulty of the effort depends on the degree to which the organization is currently using a non-bureaucratic, disciplined approach and on the resolve of management and staff to improve the way they work.

In discipline-averse and bureaucratic organizations, the effort to implement project management is more difficult. When all effort is being devoted to firefighting or handling a never-ending flow of current work and no effort is being devoted to ongoing improvement, project management is impossible. Where people reject disciplines and formality based on adolescent emotional reactions or false beliefs, there is no project management improvement.

Project management adds value but it is not free. Improving project management is a program made up of a series of projects and ongoing operational and support activities. Its critical factors are clearly understood objectives, sufficient resources, and sustained commitment.

Patience and effective communications, plus the right people with time to dedicate to the effort, are required.

What is Zen?
Historical Perspective

Zen is a form of self-investigation that began as a merging of Buddhism and Taoism. Buddhism arose in India out of Hinduism, with its nondual philosophy of Advaita and its tradition of Yoga. Taoism or "the Way" arose in China, and is closely associated with the sage Lao Tse and his focus on simplicity and experiential knowledge as opposed to complex intellectual philosophy. Taoism is not a belief-based religion. In fact, it views blind unquestioned belief as a "disease of the mind" and a root cause of strife.

Zen is a nondual tradition. That means that it has as a foundation the idea that all differences and separations, while useful for living in the material world, are not a true reflection of our basic nature. This basic nature is undifferentiated, unbounded clear space with a cognitive potential. To treat separations and differences as intrinsically real and solid is the cause of conflict.

At the heart of Buddhism is the personal discovery by the Indian Prince Siddhartha that he as an individual could overcome suffering by resting in a natural state unencumbered by wanting things to be different than they can be. After leaving his life as a wealthy and sheltered prince, he spent many years of intense austerities and work to transcend his body and the world, using the methods of the yogis of his time.

His austerities were bringing him to a state of exhaustion, but yet no closer to the realization he sought. Close to death, he remembered an experience he had as a young child in which he spontaneously felt totally active and at peace with everything as it was. This memory led him away from his austerities towards a life-sustaining path that enabled him to realize his innate potential and become a Buddha, or Awakened One. His realization was that the path to realization was a middle way that integrated and balanced extremes.

After his awakening, he taught and established a teaching tradition to help others awaken and become Buddhas. These teachings are founded on the following four "Truths"

1. There is suffering (more precisely, people experience a general sense of dissatisfaction and unease).

2. This "suffering" is caused by clinging to the desire for things to be different than they can be.

3. It is possible to eliminate suffering.

4. The path to eliminate suffering is made up of eight parts that address the cultivation of wisdom, ethical behavior, and meditation.

The Buddha was very clear in saying that these truths were not to be taken on faith or out of respect for him as a teacher but must be evaluated and put to the test until they are experientially accepted. "When you know for yourselves that, 'These these teachings are skillful; these teachings are blameless; these teachings are praised by the wise; these teachings, when adopted and carried out, lead to welfare and to happiness'—then you should enter and remain in them."—The Buddha[78]

There is *no* belief-based religion here. It is an experiment to find out whether the Buddha's experience and the teachings based on it are practical, true, and applicable to each individual. Do they work?

Taoism is the other principle influence on Zen. It is a way or process that seeks to find the way man and the course of the natural world coincide.

Taoism emphasizes various themes from the basic teachings of Taoist philosophers, such as "nonaction" (*wu wei*), *emptiness,* detachment, receptiveness, spontaneity, the strength of softness, the *relativism* of human values, and the search for a long life. The spirit in which such things are discussed tends to be more playful than doctrinaire, in keeping with the tone of the texts themselves. Taoist commentators have been very impressed by the opening lines of the Dao De Jing, which can be translated:

The way which can be uttered, is not the eternal Way.
The name which can be named, is not the eternal Name.[79]

Buddhism met Taoism in China and emerged as Chen or Chan Buddhism. Chen Buddhism was exported to Japan and gave rise to what became known in Japan as Zen, a school of Buddhism that emphasizes an unmediated awareness of the processes of the world and the mind.

In the Buddhist tradition, the highest aspiration of the practitioner is the perfection of oneself for the benefit of others. The perfected being—the Bodhisattva—does not go off into some heaven state forevermore, but returns over and over again to take human form to help others, until all beings are awakened.

Alan Watts says, "Zen Buddhism is a way and a view of life which does not belong to any of the formal categories of modern Western thought. It is not a religion or philosophy; it is not a psychology or type of science." It is a "way of liberation" or a wisdom tradition…..[80]

But even giving Zen a name takes us away from its essence. In the context of this book, we use the term loosely to encompass a relatively formless path that blends together principles of Yoga, Taoism, and Vedanta as well as elements of western psychology and systems thinking.

The wisdom traditions are not founded on belief, and do not posit a single "one right way." There is nothing to believe; no single path that must be adhered to. Instead, there is a process of letting go of the filters and conditioning that keep us from seeing things as they are.

Notes

1 "Nansen's Ordinary Mind," http://www.aikidoonline.com/index2.asp?location=/Archives/2000/oct/feat_1000_tkc.html

2   Randy Berkman, "Semantics and Zen," *Psychologia, An Intenational Journal of Psychology in the Orient,* September, 1972, from http://www.angelfire.com/wy/rvpp/semanticsandzen.html

3   http://www.brainyquote.com/quotes/quotes/a/abrahamas179907.html

4   Namkhai Norbu, *The Mirror Advice: on the Presence of Awareness*, Station Hill Openings, Barrytown Ltd., Barrytown, NY, 1996.

5   Sengstan the Third Zen Patriarch, *Verses on the Faith of Mind,* Universal Publications, Virginia Beach, VA, 1982

6   http://www.brainyquote.com/quotes/authors/s/shunryu_suzuki.html

7   Attributed to the Buddha, as taught at Insight Meditation Society, Barre, MA.

8   Alan Watts, *The Way of Zen*, p. 27.

9   Alan Watts, *The Way of Zen,* p. viii.

10   http://www.wisdomquotes.com/cat_expectations.html

11   The term Luddite is used to describe anyone opposed to *technological progress* and *technological change.* It is a reference to the Luddite social movement of the early 1800's in which textile workers in England resisted industrialization.

12   Shunryu Suzuki, *Zen Mind, Beginner's Mind*, Weatherhill; New Ed edition (April 1, 1973), p. 102

13   *www.brainyquote.com/quotes/ authors/b/benjamin_franklin.html*

14   Dr. Harold Kerzner, Best Practices Presentation , International Institute of Learning, 2004.

15   Stephen Covey, *The 8ᵗʰ Habit: From Effectiveness to Greatness*, p. 259

16 A Guide to the Project Management Body of Knowledge, Third edition, Project Maagement Institute, PA, p, 368

17 Scott Trurow, "Limitations," *The New York Times Magazine*, June 25, 2006, p.30.

18 as quoted in Thomas Cleary (Tr), *Zen Lessons: The Art of Leadership*, Shambala Publications, Boston, MA, 1989, p. 85.

19 http://www.brainyquote.com/quotes/quotes/c/charlestre172794.html.

20 http://www.virtualschool.edu/mon/Quality

21 http://www.brainyquote.com/quotes/authors/g/galen_rowell.html

22 http://www.brainyquote.com/quotes/authors/j/jeffery_veen.html

23 These are interim deliverables or artifacts. Evaluating the major artifacts in a project is called gating or "checkpointing." It is part of both quality control and financial control used to ensure that the project is on the right track and that expectations are realistic. When conditions change, these points enable decision-making regarding the continuation of the project.

24 *Matthew Yglesias Channels Roman Hruska* (Friday, June 13, 2003,

http://www. yale.edu/lawweb/jbalkin/index.htm website.)

25 Jay Lorsch and Thomas Tierney, *Aligning the Stars,* Harvard Business School Press; 1st edition (April 26, 2002), p. 25.

26 http://www.brainyquote.com/quotes/quotes/h/haroldsge113435.html

27 Stephen R. Covey, *The 8th Habit: From Effectiveness to Greatness*, Free Press; Bk & DVD edition (November 9, 2004), p. 259

28 http://www.brainyquote.com/quotes/quotes/w/wewardsd163061.html

29 http://www.brainyquote.com/quotes/quotes/a/abrahamas159011.html

30 http://www.brainyquote.com/quotes/quotes/e/edsgardijk204352.html

31 http://www.brainyquote.com/quotes/quotes/w/wewardsd133510.html

32 The Project management Institute (PMI) in the PMBOK Guide Third Edition includes quality assurance (QA) as the aspect of quality management that addresses process quality and quality control (QC). Because there are different uses of the terms quality assurance and control, we will refer specifically to process quality instead.

33 In *Blink: The Power of Thinking Without Thinking*, Malcolm Gladwell explores the phenomenon of having an immediate knowledge that is often far more accurate than the results of detailed analysis. This knowing arises out of the combination of experience, knowledge and allowing the mind to work at its internal speeds, rather than trying to control it analytically.

34 *Inquiring Mind*, Spring 2006, *"Mindfulness: The Heart of Buddhist Meditation,"* p. 5.

35 Suzuki, Shunryo, *Zen Mind Beginner's Mind*, p.38.

36 Ibid, p. 39.

37 *Inquiring Mind*, Spring 2006, p. 5

38 http://www.brainyquote.com/quotes/quotes/b/buddha118772.html

39 Peter Senge, et al, *The Fifth Discipline Fieldbook*, [Currency; 1st edition (October 1, 1994), p.6

40 http://rescomp.stanford.edu/~cheshire/EinsteinQuotes.html

41 http://www.brainyquote.com/quotes/quotes/w/williamit306493.html

42 http://maaw.info/DemingQuotes.htm

43 http://www.brainyquote.com/quotes/quotes/w/wewardsd133510.html

44 http://www.brainyquote.com/quotes/quotes/d/dalailama121172.html

45 http://www.brainyquote.com/quotes/quotes/k/kimcollins234073.html

46 http://www.worldofquotes.com/author/Robert-Burns/1/index.html

47 http://maaw.info/DemingQuotes.htm

48 www.brainydictionary.com, 2005

49 Robert Frost, "Mending Wall" , Robert Frost's Poems, St. Martin's Paperbacks (March 15, 2002), p. 94

50 Hugh Bawtree, *"How To Manage Agile/Lightweight Projects,"* *E-ssentials!*, Issue #57, Software Productivity Center Inc. (http://www.spc.ca), Nov. 2001.

51 http://www.aikidooneline.com/index2.asp?location=/Achives/ 2000/oct/feat_1000_tkc.html

52 Doen Zenji (1200-1253) the founder of Soto-Zen in Japan, from http://www.aikidoonline.com/index2.asp?location=/Archives/2000/oct/feat_1000_tkc.html

53 http://www.brainyquote.com/quotes/quotes/j/jamescashp226500.html

54 Daniel Goleman, *Emotional Intelligence: Why It Can Matter More Than IQ*, Bantam; Reprint edition (June 2, 1997, p. 161

55 http://www.brainyquote.com/quotes/quotes/i/igorsikors113146.html

56 The Tuckman/Jensen Model identifies five phases of team building: Forming, Storming, Norming, Performing, and Adjourning. Bruce W. Tuckman & Mary Ann C. Jensen, (1977). 'Stages of small group development revisited', *Group and Organizational Studies*, 2, 419-427 and M. K. Smith, (2005) ' Bruce W. Tuck-

man—Forming, Storming, Norming and Performing in Groups, *The Encyclopaedia of Informal Education*, www.infed.org/thinkers/tuckman.htm

57   http://www.wright.edu/~scott.williams/LeaderLetter/chemistry.htm

58   http://www.brainyquote.com/quotes/quotes/r/russellhe172259.html

59   Covey, *8th Habit*, p. 17.

60   Goleman, *Emotional Intelligence*, p.162

61   Covey, *8th Habit*, p 107

62   Goleman, *Emotional Intelligence* p. 292.

63   Ibid., p. 294.

64   Peter Senge, Otto Sharmer, Joseph Jaworski, and Betty Sue Flowers, *Presence: Human Purpose and the Field of the Future*, The Society for Organizational Learning, 2004, pp 11-12.

65   Ibid.

66   Mihaly Csikszentmihalyi, *Good Business*, pp 42-56

67   Tony Schwartz and Jim Loehr, *The Power of Full Engagement*: Managing Energy, Not Time, Is the Key to High Performance and Personal Renewal, Free Press; Reprint edition (December 21, 2004), *p. 5*.

68   Note that in traditional Japanese Zen, the Zazen technique is used. Here I have introduced the Insight Meditation approach because it is more structured and therefore easier for the meditator to become comfortable with the practice. In the end the methods are very similar. They lead to the same realization.

69   Tony Schwartz and Jim Loehr, *The Power of Full Engagement*: Managing Energy, Not Time, Is the Key to High Performance and Personal Renewal, Free Press; Reprint edition (December 21, 2004), 46.

70   Dharma, in Buddhism, is both the truth about the way things are, and the way it is described in scriptures. Synonyms are Torah, Tao, Truth. There are many expressions of truth, all approximating the way things *really* are.

71   A stakeholder is anyone with an interest in the project. Some stakeholders, such as project performers, clients, sponsors, suppliers or project managers, directly influence the project. Other stakeholders are influenced by the project or its outcome.

72   http://www.quoteland.com

73   *A Guide to the Project Management Body of Knowledge*, Project Management Institute, Upper Darby, PA, 1996.

74   David H. Shuster, *Teaming for Quality*, Project Management Institute, Newton Square, PA, 2000.

75   International Institute for Learning's Unified Project Management Methodology (UPMM™).

76   Portfolio management, in the PM context, is the management of multiple projects to make sure they are selected, prioritized, authorized, and controlled to achieve strategic objectives.

77   George Pitagorsky, *Managing Projects the Right Way: Key principles for successful projects*, Microsoft Corporation, 2004. All rights reserved.

78   http://www.accesstoinsight.org/tipitaka/an/an03/an03.065.than.html.

79   http://en.wikipedia.org/wiki/Taoism

80   Alan Watts, *The Way of Zen*, Pantheon Books, 1957, p. 17

Index

Form, 53–54
Formality, 166, 235
Foundation, 25–27

Goals, 38–39
 clear, 217
 definition, 39
 and objectives, 39–40
 see also Expectations; Objectives
Grounding, 11–12

Hierarchy, 201–203
 see also Teams

Improvement (continuous/ongoing),
 255–256
 and process, 145–146
Individuality, 169
Influences, 22–23
Initiating, 243–244
Insight Meditation, 222–223
Intellect, 10–11
 going beyond, 177
Intention, 22–23
Interactions, 169

Kaizen, 31
Karma, 69
Key Performance Indicators (KPI), 148
 see also Performance
Knowledge, 242
 cultivating, 128–129
 see also Performance
Koans, 11

Lao Tse, 164, 259

Management
 basics, 232–258
 definition, 234–235
 as a discipline, 257–258
 process, approximation, 233–234
 as self-inquiry, 30–31

and wisdom, 9–24,
 from your center, 209–231
 Zen, 24–37
Manifesto for Agile Software
 Development, 168–169
Mediocrity, 120
Methodologies, 164–165
 see also Performance
Mind (and awareness), 33
Mindfulness, 33–34, 89, 223–224
 and process, 136–138
Mindfulness-Based Stress Reduction
 (MBSR), 137, 223
Models (quality), 107–108
Monitoring, 253–255

Negotiating
 contract, 170–171
 definition, 55
 rational/realistic estimates, 61–62
 see also Estimating

Objectives, 38–39, 239–240
 defining, 95–96
  iteratively/realistically, 45–47
 definition, 39
 estimating, 67–69
 and goals, 39–40
 SMART, 96
 see also Expectations; Goals
Objectivity, 43–44, 150–152
Observation, 135–136
 discriminating/judgmental, 136
 self-observation, 136–138
Opinion, 44–45
Optimizing, 251
Originating, 242–243
Outcome (see Results)

Paradox, 13–14
Patience, 101–102
PDCA (Plan, Do, Check, Act), 146
Perception, 12–13